Stopping Mass Killings in Africa
Genocide, Airpower, and Intervention

Edited by

DOUGLAS C. PEIFER, PHD

Maxwell Air Force Base, Alabama

July 2008

Disclaimer

Opinions, conclusions, and recommendations expressed or implied within are solely those of the editor and do not necessarily represent the views of Air University, the United States Air Force, the Department of Defense, or any other US government agency. Cleared for public release: distribution unlimited.

Published by Books Express Publishing
Copyright © Books Express, 2010
ISBN 978-1-907521-09-6
To purchase copies at discounted prices please contact info@books-express.com

Contents

	Page
DISCLAIMER	ii
ABOUT THE EDITOR	v
PREFACE	vii
ACKNOWLEDGMENTS	xiii
Introduction to Genocide *Dr. Douglas C. Peifer*	1

Case Studies

1	American Intervention in Africa: Building on the Lessons of Somalia *Lt Col Aaron Steffens, USAF*	21
2	Genocide, Airpower, and Intervention: Rwanda 1994 *Maj George Stanley, USAF*	53
3	Defeating Genocide: An Operational Concept Based on the Rwandan Experience *Lt Col Keith Reeves, USAF*	77
4	Côte d'Ivoire: Intervention and Prevention Responses *CDR Timothy E. Boyer, USN*	101
	Conclusion *Dr. Douglas C. Peifer*	127
	CONTRIBUTORS	143
	BIBLIOGRAPHY	145
	INDEX	161

CONTENTS

Illustrations

Figure		Page
1	Hilberg's structural analysis of the destruction of the European Jews	12
2	Graphical propagation of a genocide over time	85
3	The Rwandan killing machine	90
4	Intervention trinity	95

About The Editor

Dr. Douglas C. Peifer is an associate professor in the Department of Strategy and Leadership at the US Air War College. He holds master of arts and doctor of philosophy degrees in history from the University of North Carolina at Chapel Hill, North Carolina, with a concentration in modern European diplomatic and military history. Peifer assembled this volume of case studies on operational responses to genocide as part of a project resulting from an elective he taught on the subject at the Air Command and Staff College (ACSC) in the spring of 2006. His publications include a book on *The Three German Navies*, and articles in *The Journal of Military History*, *War in History*, *War and Society*, and *The German Studies Review*. His current research focuses on European security issues; the interaction between history, culture, and foreign policy; and the challenges posed by genocide and mass killings.

Preface

This monograph seeks to contribute to the urgent task of developing realistic strategies for preventing and stopping genocide and mass killings. Neither humanitarian operations in a passive environment nor combat operations serve as appropriate models for interventions geared specifically at stopping genocide. The concept of UN Charter, chapter 7 peace enforcement operations comes closest, but US, NATO, and UN doctrine on "peace enforcement" remains sketchy and ill-defined.[1] The four case studies that comprise this monograph add an important ingredient to the literature on genocide intervention in that they provide "actionable" strategic and operational ideas. Drawing upon the experience of Somalia, Rwanda, and the Côte d'Ivoire, the authors present thoughtful recommendations for the future based on lessons derived from the past. Each case study presents an analysis of the patterns of genocide within specific historical and cultural settings, an assessment of the international and American response to deepening crises, and an array of recommendations for more effective intervention strategies compatible with limited domestic support for humanitarian interventions. All the contributors to this volume are keenly aware of and concerned about the ongoing genocide in Darfur; but given evolving developments in the region ranging from attacks on African Union (AU) peacekeepers to ongoing efforts to organize a more robust AU/UN hybrid peacekeeping operation (UN–AU Mission in Darfur), we felt that any assessment of intervention efforts in Sudan would be incomplete and partial at this time. Instead, we encourage readers to consult the Web sites of various organizations dedicated to providing timely information, analysis, and assessments of ongoing genocides, mass killings, and intervention efforts.[2] The case studies in this volume draw upon Somalia, Rwanda, and the Côte d'Ivoire rather than Darfur because these earlier crises allow historical distance, enabling assessments that will have a longer shelf life than those based on an ongoing, unfolding crisis.

Aaron Steffens' examination of the lessons of Somalia provides a set of strategic and operational lessons for more effective future responses to mass killings in Africa. Steffens bases his recommendations upon a careful examination of the complex interaction between the United Nations–led UNOSOM I and II operations and the US–led Unified Task Force (UNITAF) mission in Somalia during the period 1992 through 1994. Steffens maintains that the famine, which caused the death of some 400,000 Somalis in 1992, had as much to do with civil war and the intentional manipulation of dwindling food supplies by warlords as it did with environmental conditions. Intervention in Somalia therefore posed the same challenges as would intervention in response to future genocides or mass killings. These challenges include generating international and domestic support for action, coordinating international and national responses, and defining mission termination criteria. Steffens affirms that prevention would have been much less expensive than crisis intervention, pointing out a number of missed opportunities where the United Nations and United States failed to act. He suggests that the massive UNITAF operation (some 37,000 US troops) left troubling, unsolved problems for its less-robust UN successor, UNISOM II, setting the conditions for the October 1993 Battle of Mogadishu and the death of 18 US servicemen. Steffens' strategic and operational lessons range from the importance of prevention to the need for political solutions and the necessity to disarm locals intent on preventing conflict settlement and resolution. Steffens' discussion of how US forces can best support regional intervention forces such as the AU's African Standby Force will be of particular interest to American military personnel posted to US Africa Command, the unified military command established in 2007.[3]

The second and third case studies focus on the Rwandan genocide of April–July 1994. George Stanley poses four key questions in his analysis of Rwanda: First, why did Hutu extremists decide that genocide was a viable and effective alternative to the negotiated settlement of conflict as represented by the Arusha Peace Agreement? Second, how did the small group most committed to implementing genocide gain the necessary *active* cooperation of a broad portion of the public? Third, why did the United Nations and United States fail to intervene to prevent or stop genocide in its planning and execution phases? Lastly, *could* the United States have intervened effectively?

Drawing upon both Scott Feil's 1997 Army War College research report and Alan Kuperman's more widely disseminated 2001 book on *The Limits of Humanitarian Intervention*, Stanley concludes that intervention could have been more effective than Kuperman suggests but would have involved considerable risk.[4] He correctly notes that the French Operation Turquoise of June 1994, sometimes cited as proof that intervention would have been low risk, encountered little resistance from Hutu forces precisely because it served to prevent their opponents from overrunning the country. The reaction of Hutu extremists might have been very different 10 weeks earlier before the tide of the civil war turned clearly against them. Stanley argues that the United States should have intervened despite the risks and offers an operator's perspective on how airpower might have mitigated risks substantially, explaining how airlift, electronic jamming, reconnaissance, and direct attack might have contributed to the success of an intervention effort. Stanley's insights into the role of airpower in humanitarian and genocide-intervention operations draw upon the historical experience of Rwanda but have clear implications for future intervention strategies.

Keith Reeves' analysis of the Rwandan genocide offers a thoughtful complement to Stanley's. Reeves approaches the subject from a different angle, using Rwanda as a case study to develop a model for "rapid genocide intervention" (RGI). Reeves recognizes that preventive strategies based on the diplomatic, informational, and economic instruments of national power may be superior to military interventions in response to crisis conditions. Yet how should the US military respond to stop genocide if political leaders decide that something must be done once the killing is actually in progress? Reeves applies the tools of system analysis to the key nodes and vulnerabilities of genocide systems. His RGI concept could be implemented to disrupt or impede the process of genocide, buying valuable time for the international community and regional powers to devise long-term solutions that address underlying causes. Carefully dissecting the Rwandan killing machine to uncover its components and connections, Reeves asserts that effective intervention requires three elements. These elements, which he dubs the "intervention trinity," are rapid theater mobility, focused intelligence, and broad-based resolve. His analysis concludes with a discussion of the composition of an ideal genocide intervention force.

The final case study in this collection focuses on the successful prevention of mass killing or genocide. As Timothy Boyer points out, the Côte d'Ivoire teetered on the edge of genocide in the fall of 2002, exhibiting the same dangerous mix of ethnic tension, a civil war, and an ideology of intolerance that characterized Rwanda prior to its descent into slaughter. Boyer analyzes how certain ethnic groups were systematically excluded from power, how the media fostered hate speech, how extremist groups fostered ethnic exclusivity, and how economic disparities reinforced group tension. Yet unlike Rwanda, outside actors intervened and prevented a spiraling cycle of violence that might have degenerated into genocide. Boyer's analysis explores how France, the Economic Community of West African States, and the United Nations responded to the crisis in the Côte d'Ivoire, illustrating that under the right conditions regional and international actors other than the United States can intervene effectively. By enabling others to intervene through airpower, logistical, and communication support, the United States can promote effective intervention without directly committing US peacekeeping troops.

Stopping Mass Killings in Africa is written from the perspective of military officers who may well be tasked with translating political directives to "stop the killing" into realistic operational plans. As editor, I have included an introductory chapter defining genocide, democide, and mass killings; summarizing the key models for understanding how and when mass killings unfold; and acknowledging various efforts underway that study how best to stop mass killings. Clearly, prevention is far preferable to intervention both in terms of effectiveness and in terms of cost. Unfortunately, public awareness and support for "doing something" tends to be limited during the period when preventive actions are feasible, low-cost, and most effective. Only as the situation slips into overt mass killings does pressure build for action. The editor and contributors fully understand that an ounce of prevention is worth a pound of intervention, but contend that the US military, and the Air Force in particular, needs to be prepared to act when situations have become catastrophic. Military intervention to stop genocide should be a last resort, and pressure and assistance should be brought to bear before genocide watches and warnings become genocide emergencies. The monograph concludes with a chapter summarizing key recommendations made by Steffens, Stanley, Reeves, and Boyer, and developing some of my own thoughts on the possible role of airpower in genocide intervention operations. This monograph places a unique emphasis on the potential contributions of airpower to genocide intervention, but the officers who contributed to this collection have taken a broader perspective that explores regional and international responses where America's role may be mainly supportive. The collection will be of particular value to military officers responsible for humanitarian interventions in Africa, but will be of interest to all who seek to generate the practical solutions that will help render "never again" more than empty rhetoric.

DOUGLAS CARL PEIFER, PhD
Associate Professor, Air War College

Notes

All notes appear in shortened form. For full details, see the appropriate entry in the Bibliography.

1. See Holt and Berkman, *The Impossible Mandate?* for a sound discussion of the inadequacies of current doctrine. Joint Publication 3-07.3, *Peace Operations*, notes that peace enforcement operations should enforce sanctions and exclusion zones, restore order, forcibly separate belligerents, and conduct internment/resettlement operations. The publication provides little guidance of how to accomplish these tasks while using restraint and minimum force.

2. Reference links to some of the key organizations engaged in genocide awareness and education efforts are provided at the close of chapter 1.

3. On 6 February 2007, President Bush directed the creation of US Africa Command. For an overview of the AFRICOM mission and evolving organization, visit the command's frequently asked questions page at http://www.africom.mil/africomFAQs.asp.

4. Feil, "A Rwandan Retrospective;" Kuperman, *The Limits of Humanitarian Intervention*.

Acknowledgments

The following edited volume grew out of a 2006 seminar led by Dr. Douglas Peifer at the Air Command and Staff College at Air University, Maxwell AFB, Alabama. Initially conceived as an academic seminar analyzing the causes, conduct, and consequences of genocide and mass killing, the seminar embraced the challenge of exploring how the US military might contribute to genocide prevention. The interplay between Peifer's academic background in history and Holocaust studies and the operational expertise of mid-career Air Force and Navy pilots, logisticians, and combat support specialists made for lively, informed discussions about operational responses to genocide and mass killings. The contributors to this volume would like to thank their peers and professors at ACSC for providing an environment that enabled discussion and research on issues that fall outside the mainframe of professional military studies.

Given the frequent deployments and high-tempo operations of today's military professionals, the student scholars whose papers were selected for publication extend a particular word of thanks to their families. Aaron Steffens thanks his two beautiful girls, Jennifer and Samantha, for their unfailing support. Keith Reeves thanks his ever-supportive wife and best friend, Tess, for listening to his endless griping about writer's block, and his daughters, Jessica and Jalen, for reminding him of the important things in life. Tim Boyer owes a debt of gratitude to his lovely wife, Lisa, for her support and encouragement and to the friendly and patient staff at the AU library in helping work through the maze of reference material. George Stanley would like to thank his beautiful wife, Londa, and his wonderful children, Scott and Alena, for their patience and faithful encouragement during this research project. All four thank Dr. Peifer for his enthusiastic support and guidance during the seminar, while researching and writing, and throughout the publication process.

Douglas Peifer would like to thank all the members of the 2006 seminar on "Genocide and Intervention" for their insights and contributions. At Air University, he would like to thank Chris Cain, Shirley Laseter, Dan Mortensen, Stephen Burgess,

ACKNOWLEDGMENTS

Kevin Holzimmer, and others for pushing this project forward. Special thanks to James Howard and Darlene Barnes for their unstinting support in editing and preparing the manuscript. Peifer would like to single out Gerhard Weinberg for stimulating his interest in genocide studies and Zev Weiss for enabling his participation in Northwestern University's Summer Institute on the Holocaust. Last but not least, he thanks Beth, his parents, and his four wonderful sons for their support and love.

Introduction to Genocide

Dr. Douglas C. Peifer

Never again. Two words capture the grim determination of Holocaust survivors that the world should never forget what happened and never allow another cold-blooded murder of millions based on their religion, ethnicity, race, or national origin. Following Raul Hilberg's groundbreaking *Destruction of the European Jews* in 1961 and the trial of Adolf Eichmann that same year, a dense network of scholars, university programs, foundations, and museums slowly developed to ensure that the Holocaust or Shoah would never be forgotten and to examine the causes and conditions that allowed it to happen.[1] Parallel efforts emerged dedicated to understanding the Armenian genocide, the destruction of Native Americans, and other mass killings. Yet despite these efforts, the international community stood by and allowed genocide to unfold in Cambodia, in Bosnia, in Rwanda, and elsewhere during the closing decades of the twentieth century. The twenty-first century has proved equally disturbing thus far, with perhaps as many as 400,000 lives extinguished in Darfur and some 2.3 million Darfuris displaced by the violence.[2] Genocide Watch, an international group dedicated to raising awareness of and influencing public policies toward potential and actual genocides, lists one genocide in progress (Darfur), one region where genocide is deemed imminent (Chad), and four areas exhibiting warning signs of possible mass killings (Burma, Kenya, Uzbekistan, and Zimbabwe) as of January 2008.[3]

Outraged by the inaction of nations and the international community to the killing fields of Cambodia, the Rwandan genocide of 1994, the slaughter of some 7,000 Bosnian Muslim men and boys at Srebrenica in July 1995, and the deteriorating situation in Kosovo in the late 1990s, concerned individuals and organizations began to network and become more active in generating pressure to prevent future genocides. The United States Holocaust Memorial Museum (USHMM) established a Committee on Conscience, charged with alerting the national conscience, influencing policy makers, and stimulating worldwide action to confront and halt genocide, mass killings, and related crimes against humanity.[4] Samantha Power, a war correspondent, pricked America's conscience with her frontline articles the Balkans during the 1990s and a best-selling 2002 book *A Problem from Hell: America and the Age of Genocide*.[5] Gregory Stanton, an international human rights lawyer who worked for the US Department of State's Office of Cambodian Genocide Investigations, founded Genocide Watch. Existing nongovernmental organizations such as Refugees International became increasingly concerned about the overlap between humanitarian assistance, war, and genocide. Last but not least, universities became ever more engaged in genocide studies, with institutes and centers such as the Montreal Institute for Genocide and Human Rights Studies and Yale University's Genocide Studies Program generating both scholarship and activism.[6] Not surprisingly, among the most vocal voices pressing the US government and the United Nations for action were student groups such as Students Taking Action Now: Darfur (STAND), whose chapters have organized dozens of rallies, vigils, and teach-ins about Darfur since the first chapter was founded at Georgetown University in 2004.[7]

As journalists, citizen coalitions, student-action groups, university centers, and policy institutes generated public awareness of mass killings and genocides, American politicians responded. On the Republican side, Pres. George W. Bush included genocide among the security challenges he addressed in his 2002 *National Security Strategy* and elevated the issue in his 2006 *National Security Strategy*.[8] Devoting an entire page to the issue, President Bush warned that:

> It is a moral imperative that states take action to prevent and punish genocide. History teaches that sometimes other states will not act unless America does its part. We must refine United States Government efforts—economic, diplomatic, and law-enforcement—so that they target those individuals responsible for genocide and not the innocent citizens they rule. Where perpetrators of mass killing defy all attempts at peaceful intervention, armed intervention may be required, preferably by the forces of several nations working together under appropriate regional or international auspices.
>
> We must not allow the legal debate over the technical definition of "genocide" to excuse inaction. The world must act in cases of mass atrocities

and mass killing that will eventually lead to genocide even if the local parties are not prepared for peace.[9]

President Bush was not the only voice in the Republican camp taking up the issue. Others, such as Senator Sam Brownback of Kansas and Rep. Henry Hyde of Illinois, have been deeply engaged in seeking solutions to the Darfur crisis.[10] On the Democratic side, representatives Tom Lantos (California) and Michael Capuano (Maryland) have sponsored legislation on the issue, with Joseph Biden (Delaware), Richard Durbin (Illinois), Hillary Clinton (New York), and Joseph Lieberman (Connecticut) tackling the issue in the Senate.[11] While activists have unhappily noted that mass killings continue in Darfur and threaten to unfold in southern Sudan, Somalia, and elsewhere, the president's appointment of a Special Envoy to Sudan (Andrew Natsios, September 2006–December 2007, and subsequently Richard Williamson) stands in stark contrast to the US hands-off policy during the Rwandan genocide.[12] Seeking to generate concrete "practical recommendations to enhance the US government's capacity to respond to emerging threats of genocide and mass atrocities," former secretary of state Madeleine Albright and former secretary of defense William Cohen announced in November 2007 the creation of a Genocide Prevention Task Force. Madeleine Albright's opening statement captures the problems that policy makers face when confronted with mass killings: "The world agrees that genocide is unacceptable and yet genocide and mass killings continue. Our challenge is to match words to deeds and stop allowing the unacceptable. That task, simple on the surface, is in fact one of the most persistent puzzles of our times. We have a duty to find the answer before the vow of 'never again' is once again betrayed."[13]

Defining Genocide

Raphael Lemkin first coined the term "genocide" in 1944 as he struggled to convey Nazi extermination policies in his book *Axis Rule in Occupied Europe*.[14] Born in what was the Polish portion of the Russian Empire, young Lemkin had grown up under the shadow of pogrom and persecution as a Polish Jew. Graduating from Lvov law school in the 1920s, he felt drawn to the topic of mass killings, studying the fate of the Armenians and of the Assyrian minority in Iraq. Well before the contours of the Holocaust became apparent, Lemkin proposed at a conference in 1933 that the League of Nations should ban the "crime of barbarity," which he defined as the "premeditated destruction of national, racial, religious, and social collectives."[15] The rise of the Nazi party in Germany and deepening anti-Semitism throughout Eastern Europe signaled that the topic was of more than academic interest. When the Wehrmacht stormed into Poland in 1939, Lemkin sought refuge first in Sweden and then in the United States. Deeply concerned about the fate of those now under German rule, he devoted himself to assembling the laws, orders, and decrees that chronicled Nazi policy toward Europe's occupied peoples, particularly its Jews. His massive 712-page study sought to document Nazi policy, and introduced the term *genocide* into the English vocabulary.[16]

At Nuremberg and in various postwar trials, the Allies had charged and prosecuted German organizations and individuals with planning, initiating, and waging wars of aggression; conspiring to commit crimes against peace; committing war crimes; and committing crimes against humanity. Lemkin advised the US chief counsel at the Nuremberg Trials and continued to campaign for an international law criminalizing genocide. In December 1946, the General Assembly of the young United Nations passed a resolution condemning genocide and tasking a committee to draft an international treaty banning it.

Committee members engaged with drafting the convention devoted much discussion and debate to defining genocide. What distinguished genocide from other forms of mass death, such as famine or war? How should the crime be defined so that the Soviets—guilty of their own mass murders—would not obstruct the treaty?[17] And how could the treaty be made meaningful as a measure designed to stop the process of mass killing rather than simply punish those responsible after its completion?

By 1948 the committee had completed its task. Articles 2 and 3 of the Convention on the Prevention and Punishment of the Crime of Genocide defined both the concept of genocide and what acts would be deemed punishable:

Article 2

In the present Convention, genocide means any of the following acts committed with intent to destroy, in whole or in part, a national, ethnical, racial or religious group, as such:

  (a) Killing members of the group;
  (b) Causing serious bodily or mental harm to members of the group;
  (c) Deliberately inflicting on the group conditions of life calculated to bring about its physical destruction in whole or in part;
  (d) Imposing measures intended to prevent births within the group;
  (e) Forcibly transferring children of the group to another group.

Article 3

The following acts shall be punishable:

  (a) Genocide;
  (b) Conspiracy to commit genocide;
  (c) Direct and public incitement to commit genocide;
  (d) Attempt to commit genocide;
  (e) Complicity in genocide.[18]

The effectiveness of the Convention on the Prevention and Punishment of the Crime of Genocide has been limited. Adopted by a resolution of the General Assembly in December 1948, the convention required ratification by 20 members of the United Nations before coming into force. By October 1950, 20 states had ratified the convention, but the United States was not among them. Initially, the American Bar Association and southern senators opposed the treaty due to the ambiguities of article 2. Later, conservatives opposed the convention due to concerns about US sovereignty. But its supporters never abandoned the issue, with Senator William Proxmire delivering some 3,211 speeches on the topic between 1967 and 1986.[19] With Pres. Ronald Reagan's strong support, the Senate finally ratified the convention in 1986, dragging its feet another two years before passing the Genocide Convention Implementation Act in October 1988.

After exerting little influence for 40-odd years, the Convention on the Prevention and Punishment of the Crime of Genocide became an important reference point for tribunals, courts, and legal cases in the 1990s and twenty-first century. The International Criminal Tribunal for the former Yugoslavia, the International Criminal Tribunal for Rwanda, the International Court of Justice, and the International Criminal Court have all tried perpetrators of genocide, drawing upon the convention's definition of genocide. Yet Lemkin, Proxmire, and others had hoped that the Convention would be an effective tool for preventing genocide, with article 8 calling the "United Nations to take such action under the Charter of the United Nations as they consider appropriate for the prevention and suppression of acts of genocide or any of the other acts enumerated in article 3."

Here the record is less encouraging. During the Cold War, the international community made no effort to invoke the convention while Mao Tse-tung's Great Leap Forward and Cultural Revolution killed millions of Chinese between 1958 and 1968, when Suharto's anticommunist campaign in Indonesia targeted entire villages for liquidation in 1965–66, when Pakistan's civil war veered toward genocidal mayhem in 1971, or when the Khmer Rouge eliminated an estimated 20 percent of the Cambodian population between 1975 and 1979.[20] The US accession to the convention in 1988 and the end of the Cold War did not render the international community any more effective at stopping mass killings, with some 800,000 Tutsis slaughtered by Hutu extremists in Rwanda in April–July 1994 and with UN peacekeepers helplessly looking on the next year as Serb forces rounded up some 7,000 Bosnian men and boys for execution at Srebrenica.[21] Indeed, during the Rwandan genocide, the State Department and National Security Council deliberately avoided using the term genocide precisely because they feared that use of the term might compel some sort of action.[22]

This fear proved misplaced. In 1995 and 1999 NATO intervened to stop ethnic cleansing and war in Bosnia and Kosovo, subsequently stationing robust peacekeeping forces in the region. Sickened by the violence on NATO's doorstep and fearful that further inaction would undermine the alliance's credibility, European and American leaders responded out of both perceived national interest and humanitarian concern without directly invoking the genocide convention. Ten years after the Rwandan genocide, the United Nations and the United States began to directly invoke the term as the killings in the Darfur region of Sudan mounted. On 7 April 2004,

UN secretary general Kofi Annan announced an Action Plan to Prevent Genocide, subsequently appointing a Special Advisor on Genocide Prevention.[23] Later that year, the US secretary of state, Colin Powell, specifically termed the crisis in Darfur a genocide.[24] Yet only after protracted and difficult negotiations did the contours of an effective intervention force become apparent. In July 2007, UN Security Council Resolution (UNSCR) 1769 was unanimously adopted, authorizing a joint United Nations–African Union (UN–AU) peacekeeping force with a projected number of some 20,000 troops, more than 6,000 police, and a significant civilian component.[25] Three years had elapsed between Annan's "Action Plan" and the UN resolution. Despite rhetorical support for stopping genocide from the White House and the State Department, as of January 2008 UN–AU mission in Darfur, (UNAMID), the joint African Union/United Nations hybrid operation that replaced the African Union operation in Darfur, still lacks helicopters. UN secretary general Ban Ki-moon remarked that "In the past weeks and months, I have contacted, personally, every possible contributor of helicopters—in the Americas, in Europe, in Asia. And yet, not one helicopter has been made available yet."[26]

The Convention on the Prevention and Punishment of the Crime of Genocide clearly defines genocide and associated acts in articles 1 and 2, and opens the door for contracting parties to "call upon the competent organs of the United Nations to take such action under the Charter of the United Nations as they consider appropriate for the prevention and suppression of acts of genocide or any of the other acts enumerated in article 3."[27] Yet the treaty has been disappointing in its effect: for much of the Cold War, nations simply ignored the convention and even during the post–Cold War era, signatories have been slow and reluctant to put speedy and effective intervention forces at the United Nations' disposal. Despite this, the treaty should not be dismissed as entirely ineffective: the special tribunals set up by the United Nations to try responsible parties for crimes of genocide, war crimes, and gross infractions of international law may well exert a deterrent effect on groups contemplating mass murder.

The Related Concepts Democide and Politicide

The concept of genocide is useful, communicating the intent to exterminate people for who they are rather than what they do. By using the term *genocide*, one conveys that people are being targeted because of their membership in a group rather than because of any particular action on their part. In war, enemy soldiers and combatants are targeted because of their contributions to the enemy's war effort. Theoretically, once soldiers have surrendered or once combatant civilians (those working in arms factories, etc.) cease contributing to their nation's war effort, they become noncombatants and are no longer legitimate targets of war. In genocide the targeted individual typically does not have this option: Turks targeted Armenians simply because they were Armenians, Nazis targeted Jews simply because they were Jews, and Hutus targeted Tutsis because they were Tutsi.

In framing the legal definition of genocide, those drafting the genocide convention restricted the concept of group identity to national, ethnical, racial, or religious groups. Given that the Soviets would have blocked any measure that broadened the concept to include political and social groups, this was unavoidable at the time the convention was framed in the late 1940s. Thus Stalinist killings, Indonesian massacres, and Mao's bloody repressions did not fall within the legal definition of genocide. Yet since the end of the Cold War, academics, journalists, politicians, and the general public have tended to use the term more broadly and include mass killings based on other forms of group identity. Comparative studies of genocide typically include the Stalinist extermination of the Kulaks, the Khmer Rouge elimination of intellectuals and city dwellers, and Mao's mass killings.[28] A number of authors have pushed the concept further to include political murder, such as Argentina's dirty war, and even strategic air campaigns that have targeted civilians.[29]

R. J. Rummel, a political scientist, has noted the discrepancy between the treaty definition of genocide, the expanded popular conception of the term, and related mass killings. He proposes that we adopt an alternative term, *democide*, encompassing genocide ("the killing of people by a government because of their indelible group membership"), politicide ("the murder of any person or people by a government because of their politics or for political purposes"), and mass murder ("the indiscriminate killing of any person or people by a government"). Rummel's influential *Death by Government* (1994) and *Statistics of Democide: Genocide and Mass Murder since 1900* (1995) provide statistical examinations of each of these categories, arriving at the chilling conclusion that perhaps 262 million people died as a result of democide in the twentieth century.[30] Rummel correctly argues that one should include politicide alongside genocide in assessing government-sanctioned mass murder. Yet by arguing that civilians and prisoners of war killed by starvation, indiscriminate bombing and shelling, and neglect during times of war are victims of mass murder rather than war, Rummel obscures the reality that war has always encompassed deaths beyond the battlefield.[31] The sieges of antiquity, Genghis Khan's use of terror as a tool, British and German attempts to cut the flow of food to each other in both world wars, and the concept of nuclear deterrence all encompassed death beyond the battlefield.

Rummel's key finding—that totalitarian regimes engage in more democidal behavior than democratic regimes—lends itself to misuse as a policy prescription.[32] For Rummel, democide, war, and even famine have one simple solution, freedom: "To foster freedom is to foster a solution to war and democide, and to minimize domestic collective violence."[33] Promoting democracy as a long-term strategy may decrease the frequency of war and democide, but the jury is still out on the subject.[34] As a preventive and interventionist tool, stopping democide by the forcible overthrow of a regime has proven costly, ineffective, and diplomatically isolating. Addressing the goal of preventing and stopping genocide will prove difficult enough, but in contrast with the neoconservative agenda, that goal enjoys broad international support, with over 130 countries having publicly committed themselves to the undertaking.[35]

Recognizing the Stages and Likelihood of Genocide and Mass Killings

In order to prevent and stop genocide, one has to recognize its warning signs. This entails understanding the stages and steps towards genocide, assessing the likelihood of genocide, and then formulating preventive and interventionist responses. The Genocide Intervention Network, the USHMM Committee on Conscience, Genocide Watch, Prevent Genocide International, and various other nongovernmental organizations now issue specific alerts regarding potential and ongoing genocides, joining organizations with a broader mandate such as the International Red Cross, Amnesty International, and Human Rights Watch.[36] The Genocide Intervention Network and the USHMM Committee on Conscience do so by providing action alerts and listing areas of concern. Genocide Watch ranks crises as genocide emergencies when "genocide is actually under way," genocide warnings when "politicide or genocide is imminent," and genocide watches when "early warning signs indicate the danger of mass killing or genocide."[37]

The concept of analyzing genocide structurally and identifying its stages owes much to pioneering studies of the Holocaust. Raul Hilberg's *The Destruction of the European Jews* has proven particularly influential.[38] Hilberg, like Lemkin, fled Nazi rule and settled in the United States. He attended Abraham Lincoln High School in Brooklyn, served in the US Army, and participated in the US Army's War Documentation, which assembled German records for use in postwar trials and for historical purposes.[39] His Columbia dissertation (1955) broke new ground by analyzing the structure and process of the Final Solution. Five publishers turned down the manuscript due to its length and subject matter, but since its initial publication in 1961, Hilberg's work has become an essential, if controversial, reference point.[40]

The Destruction of the European Jews provoked debate because it asserted that traditional Jewish strategies for dealing with force and persecution had failed disastrously during the 1930s and 1940s. Hilberg noted that many German policies, ranging from laws banning Jews from certain jobs to decrees assembling them into ghettos to requirements for distinct clothing, had historical precedence. He asserted that Jewish communities had over the centuries focused on alleviating the impact of discriminatory policies while generally complying with rather than confronting state policies. This tendency toward alleviation, evasion, paralysis, and compliance rather than resistance served Jewish communities well during the medieval and early modern period, but Hilberg claimed that it failed to recognize the contours of the process of genocide.[41] And it is here that Hilberg has been most influential: his discussion of the structure of destruction laid a model for understanding how the Holocaust had been very different from the pogroms, massacres, and communal violence to which Jewish people had been long subjected.

Hilberg concluded that the Final Solution involved a number of steps. First, the Nazi state had to define who was a Jew. This initial step proved more complicated than anticipated, in that Nazi racial ideology had abandoned religious definitions of Jew and Christian in favor of racial categories of Jew and Aryan. If laws banning Jewish employment and ownership were to be enforced, lawyers would have to clarify the status of children of mixed ancestry, determine whether exceptions should be made for Jewish veterans, and decide whether or not converted Jews should be subjected to these policies. Next, Jews found themselves the targets of expropriation, as Jewish firms were seized, as special taxes and levies were passed, and as family property and savings were confiscated. Expropriation led to concentration, as Jews were turned out of their houses, crowded into ghettoes, and exploited as forced labor. Concentration in turn enabled more efficient annihilation, whether by mobile killing operations, by working Jews to death, or by the industrialized process of gassing large groups in specially designed gas chambers.

Hilberg's structural analysis of the destruction of Europe's Jews, laid out in figure 1, has been adopted and disseminated widely. Clearly laying out the stages and steps involved in the murder of some six million European Jews, Hilberg provided a structural analysis to which others have turned in seeking to understand other mass killings and genocides.

Hilberg's model seeks to explain the stages that led to the Holocaust, a uniquely modern horror which prompted Lemkin

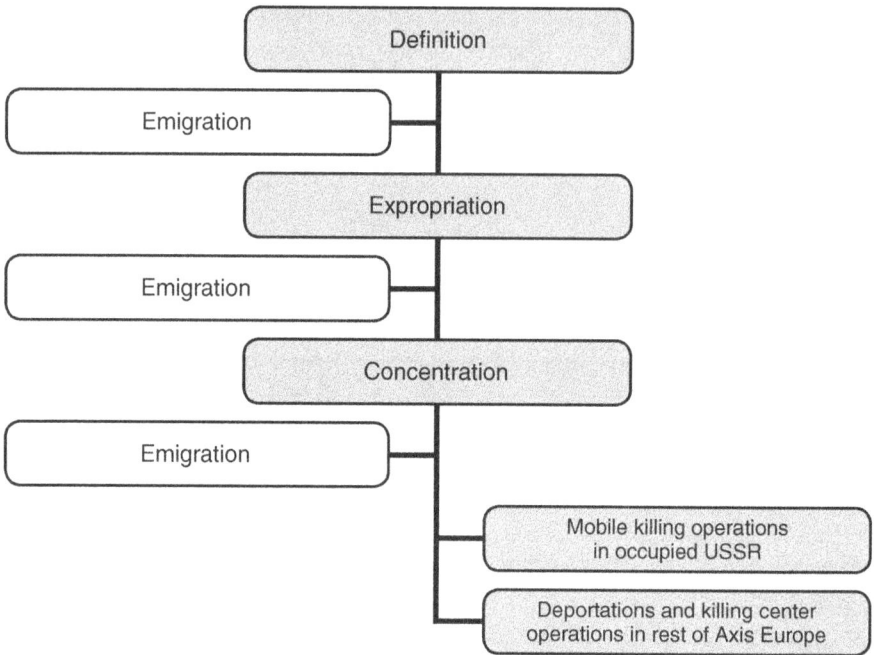

Figure 1. Hilberg's structural analysis of the destruction of the European Jews. Adapted from Raul Hilberg, *The Destruction of the European Jews*. (London: W. H. Allen, 1961).

to conceive of the term *genocide*. Since its publication, the world has experienced additional mass killings, establishing the necessity for a broader, more general model for understanding genocide. Gregory Stanton, drawn to the field of genocide studies due to his early involvement in examining the Cambodian killing fields, has proposed the following schema, noting that "prevention of genocide requires a structural understanding of the genocidal process."[42] Stanton believes that genocides typically develop through eight states as described below:

Classification

Distinguishing between different groups of people, establishing "us" and "them" categories.

Symbolization

Identifying certain symbols with out groups, using either customary dress or government imposed identifying symbols or distinctive clothing.

Dehumanization

Associating targeted groups with repellent animals or microbes. Stanton gives the examples of Nazis calling Jews "vermin," Rwandan Hutu hate radio referring to Tutsis as "cockroaches."

Organization

Formation of groups and institutions ranging from mobs to militias to advanced bureaucracies that support and implement the genocide process.

Polarization

The deliberate, systematic effort to cut social connections between targeted groups and the broader society. Stanton notes that "the first to be killed in a genocide are moderates from the killing group who oppose the extremists."

Preparation

Stanton borrows from Hilberg, noting that preparation involves identifying those targeted, expropriating their property, concentrating the victims, and in the most extreme cases, building facilities for extermination.

Extermination

Killing the targeted out group.

Denial

Stanton adds an eighth stage, denial, to the process. He notes that typically records of the killing are burned, international accusations dismissed, and efforts are made to cover up the killings.[43]

As president of Genocide Watch, Stanton combines the attributes of activist, advocate, and scholar. His schema, fully developed on Genocide Watch's Web site, provides a conceptual model for understanding genocide, with Stanton providing examples of preventive measures that can be taken at each step.

Barbara Harff, a political scientist at the US Naval Academy, has added to our understanding of the genocide process by analyzing its causal factors. Using a comparative, empirical approach, Harff has sought to identify key factors that should provide warning signs of possible genocide. The factors she identifies as contributing to its occurrence include: (1) prior incidents of genocide or politicide in the region, (2) a high degree of political upheaval, (3) a ruling elite defined in terms of ethnicity, (4) a "belief system that . . . justifies efforts to restrict, persecute, or eliminate certain categories of people," (5) an autocratic form of government, and (6) a trade system opposed to openness.[44]

Harff notes that her social scientific approach is "not enough to tell us . . . precisely when genocidal violence is likely to begin," but she believes that an effort to systematically assess the risk of genocide improves the prospects for prevention and early response. Her work moves beyond Hilberg and Stanton's work of analyzing *how* genocide takes place, and engages the question of *why* genocide occurs.

Prevention and the Responsibility to Protect

Survivors, scholars, and activists have pushed our understanding of genocide and mass killings a good deal further than the legalistic definitions of the genocide convention. We now have well-researched models that explain mass killings as a process and identify the factors that contribute to its onset. Numerous organizations provide updates on global areas of concern, issuing watches, warnings, and emergency declarations. Yet despite this knowledge, it has become clear that information alone provides neither the impetus to intervene nor guidance on how to prevent or stop mass killing. A growing community of individuals, think tanks, and governments now advocate that the international community's has the "responsibility to protect" (R2P). Rather than focusing on specific terminology, proponents of R2P argue that the international community has the responsibility to protect civilians when states fail to do so themselves. Whether victims of genocide, ethnic cleansing, intentional famine, or indiscriminate war, civilians subjected to mass killing have a right to protection. And when their governments and rulers fail to provide that basic right, then the international community has the responsibility and duty to do so.[45]

Secretary General Kofi Annan, who headed the United Nations' Department of Peacekeeping Operations during the Rwandan genocide, appointed a panel in 2000 tasked with undertaking "a thorough review of the United Nations peace and security activities" and presenting a "clear set of specific, concrete and practical recommendations to assist the United Nations."[46] Among its recommendations, the panel advised that the United Nations should develop its "ability to fully deploy traditional peacekeeping operations within 30 days of the adoption of a Security Council resolution establishing such an operation, and within 90 days in the case of complex peacekeeping operations." Moreover, UN peacekeepers who witnessed violence against civilians were to presume that they were authorized to intervene.

While the panel thereby recognized the responsibility of UN peacekeepers to protect civilians from violence, it cautioned "the United Nations does not wage war. Where enforcement action is required, it has consistently been entrusted to coalitions of willing States, with the authorization of the Security Council, acting under Chapter VII of the Charter."[47]

Given that genocide occurs most frequently during times of war—either because perpetrators use the cover of war to justify eliminating racial, religious, or political groups or as part of a counterinsurgency—the UN model of chapter 6 peacekeeping operations is inappropriate. Noting that chapter 7 enforcement actions would fall to coalitions of the willing, the Canadian government established an International Commission on Intervention and State Sovereignty (ICISS) in September 2000. The commission's report, issued in December 2001, has become the blueprint for the concept of R2P.

Citing the experience and aftermath of Somalia, Rwanda, Srebrenica, and Kosovo, the ICISS asserted that "when a particular state is clearly either unwilling or unable to fulfill its responsibility to protect or is itself the actual perpetrator of crimes or atrocities" the broader community of states has a responsibility to intervene. The commission broke down the responsibility to protect into preventive, reactive, and rebuilding components, seeking to change the terms of the international debate on intervention from right to responsibility.

The ICISS report has spurred numerous ongoing efforts that seek to explore how, when, by whom, and under what authorization protective interventions should take place. In the United States, the Henry L. Stimson Center in Washington, DC, has a vibrant program exploring "The Future of Peace Operations."[48] Harvard's Carr Center for Human Rights Policy and the US Army's Peacekeeping and Stability Operations Institute are cooperating on the Mass Atrocity Response Operations Project, which seeks to develop "credible and realistic operational planning for responding to genocide and mass atrocity."[49] Most recently, the United States Holocaust Memorial Museum, the American Academy of Diplomacy, and the United States Institute of Peace convened a Genocide Prevention Task Force charged with issuing a report on genocide prevention and intervention by December 2008.[50] The concept of R2P is gathering momentum, shifting the focus of debate from the legalities of the genocide convention to the practicalities of prevention and intervention. R2P is ambitious, advocating that the community of states intervenes when one of its members fails to protect its own citizens, is the agent of ethnic cleansing, genocide, or the deliberate targeting of civilian populations in times of war. Preventing and stopping genocide, broadly defined, would be a first, important step toward a world where mass murderers cannot hide behind the veil of state sovereignty.

One can take two approaches to devising strategies for preventing and stopping mass killings. One approach is to think in terms of generic scenarios and broad, general strategies. This approach might be termed the doctrine approach where generally accepted best practices are promulgated to be adapted as called for by the specific situation. Another approach, most suitable when there are no generally accepted best practices, is the historical approach. Context rich, the historical approach looks at specific scenarios, examines the historical record, and advances recommendations based on concrete case studies. This monograph takes the second approach, trusting that a full understanding of context and culture is required in devising strategies of prevention and intervention.

Notes

All notes appear in shortened form. For full details, see the appropriate entry in the Bibliography.

1. Hilberg, *The Destruction of the European Jews*, 1961.
2. Save Darfur Coalition, "September Briefing Paper."
3. "News Monitors," *Genocide Watch*, http://www.genocidewatch.org/resources/newsmonitors.html (accessed 28 January 2008).
4. The United States Holocaust Memorial Museum's Committee on Conscience maintains a Web site on "Responding to Threats of Genocide Today" at http://www.ushmm.org/conscience/.
5. Power, *A Problem from Hell*. Power now teaches at Harvard's John F. Kennedy School of Government, where she was the founding executive director of the Carr Center for Human Rights Policy.
6. Visit the Web sites of the Montreal Institute for Genocide and Human Rights Studies and Yale University's Genocide Studies Program (http://migs.concordia.ca/ and http://www.yale.edu/gsp/) for a sense of the interaction between scholarship and activism. Dozens of other universities have established or expanded genocide programs and institutes, among them Northwestern University, the University of Vermont, the University of Minnesota, and the University of Nevada at Reno. For a sense of the number of programs, see Yale University's links to genocide programs at http://www.yale.edu/gsp/links/index.html.
7. For a history of Students Taking Action Now: Darfur and its current campaigns, see http://standnow.org/. While still dedicated to generating support for action in Darfur, the student group has renamed itself the Student Anti-Genocide Coalition, and has become this generation's equivalent to the antiapartheid student movement of the 1980s.
8. The White House, *The National Security Strategy*, 2002, 6. http://www.whitehouse.gov/nsc/nss/2002/index.html.
9. The White House, *The National Security Strategy*, 2006, 17. Bush reemphasized that the United States opposes genocide in his State of the Union speech of 28 January 2008, transcript available at http://www.whitehouse.gov/news/releases/2008/01/20080128-13.html (accessed 29 January 2008).
10. See Jerry Fowler's interview with Senator Brownback on *Vital Voices on Genocide Prevention*, a podcasting service of the United States Holocaust Memorial Museum at http://www.ushmm.org/conscience/analysis/details.php?content=2005-11-24 (podcast, 24 November 2005).
11. For a summary of antigenocide acts, resolutions, and amendments passed or pending in the House and Senate, consult DarfurScore.org's Web

site which grades representatives and senators on their contributions to stopping genocide. The scorecard, sponsored by Genocide Intervention Network, can be accessed at http://www.darfurscores.org/darfur-legislation.

12. See the Department of State press release of 19 September 2006 regarding Andrew Natsios appointment at http://www.state.gov/r/pa/prs/ps/2006/72830.htm.

13. US Holocaust and Memorial Museum press release, 13 November 2007, on the establishment of the Genocide Prevention Task Force, available at http://www.ushmm.org/conscience/taskforce/press/?content=2007-11-13. The task force includes Senator John Danforth, Senator Tom Daschle, Amb Stuart Eizenstat, Mr. Michael Gerson, Secretary Dan Glickman, Secretary Jack Kemp, Judge Gabrielle Kirk McDonald, Amb Tom Pickering, Ms. Julia Taft, Mr. Vin Weber, and Gen Anthony Zinni.

14. Lemkin, *Axis Rule in Occupied Europe.*

15. Power, *A Problem from Hell*, 21.

16. Ibid., 21, 38–40.

17. Weiss-Wendt, "Hostage of Politics," 552.

18. United Nations, "Convention on the Prevention and Punishment of the Crime of Genocide."

19. Power, *A Problem from Hell*, 166.

20. Kiernan, "The Cambodian Genocide—1975–1979," 348.

21. Totten, Parsons, and Charny, *Century of Genocide*, 265.

22. The guidelines reportedly instructed government spokesmen to only use the term "acts of genocide" rather than genocide. Orentlicher, "Genocide," 2.

23. Annan, "Action Plan to Prevent Genocide."

24. Robert McMahon, "UN: Powell Calls Darfur Atrocities 'Genocide.'"

25. Peace and Security Section, the United Nations Department of Public Information, "The United Nations and Darfur."

26. Ibid.

27. United Nations, "Convention on the Prevention and Punishment of the Crime of Genocide."

28. See for examples Kiernan, *Blood and Soil*; Totten, Bartrop, and Jacobs, *Dictionary of Genocide*; Totten, Parsons, and Charny, *Century of Genocide*; Valentino, *Final Solutions*; and Weitz, *A Century of Genocide*.

29. Hewitt's reader *Defining the Horrific*, designed for undergraduate courses on genocide, includes a chapter on Argentina and Guatemala as well as a chapter on the atomic bomb.

30. Rummel, *Death by Government*; and Rummel, *Statistics of Democide*. Rummel continues to update and change his estimates of civilian deaths at his Web site at the University of Hawaii at http://www.hawaii.edu/powerkills/welcome.html.

31. Rummel has argued that war has not been the twentieth century's biggest killer, but makes this case by comparing battlefield deaths against democide. He places the myriad noncombatant casualties of war—helpless people killed in time of war, prisoners of war detained under conditions that cause their death, civilians killed as a result of indiscriminate bombing, or the starvation of civilians in time of war—under the category mass murder.

Granted, the number of people killed by genocide, democide, and mass murder greatly exceeds those killed on the battlefield. But war's death toll extends beyond the battlefield, with the Geneva conventions often ignored by belligerents, hence in☐ating the casualties of democide. Rummel, "Chapter 2: Definition of Democide."

32. Rummel supported Bush's "forward strategy of freedom" in 2003 and remains adamant in his support of the "democratic peace thesis." See his postings on the subject at http://www.hawaii.edu/powerkills/COMM.12.1.03.HTM.

33. The quote from the introduction of R. J. Rummel's Freedom's Principles is available at http://www.hawaii.edu/powerkills/FREEDOM'S.PRINCIPLES.HTM. For a more elaborate development of his idea that freedom is the cure for war, democide, and famine, see Rummel, *Never Again*.

34. For a critique of the democratic peace thesis, see Henderson, *Democracy and War*.

35. Prevent Genocide International lists 137 members as having ratified the Convention on the Prevention and Punishment of the Crime of Genocide. Prevent Genocide International, "Information on the Genocide Convention."

36. See also http://www.genocidewatch.org/ and http://www.genocideintervention.net/.

37. Genocide Watch, "Genocide Watch has three levels of Genocide Alerts®."

38. Hilberg, *The Destruction of the European Jews*, 1985.

39. Hilberg obituary, *International Herald Tribune*.

40. Martin, "Raul Hilberg."

41. Hilberg, *The Destruction of the European Jews*, 1985, 22.

42. Stanton, "The Eight Stages of Genocide," 1996.

43. Ibid., 1998.

44. Harff, "Assessing Risks of Genocide and Politicide." For a more developed assessment, see Harff, "No Lessons Learned from the Holocaust?"

45. For a detailed discussion of the origins and trajectory of the "responsibility to protect" (R2P) movement, see Holt and Berkman, *The Impossible Mandate?*

46. United Nations, "Report of the Panel on United Nations Peace Operations."

47. Ibid., 10.

48. The Henry L. Stimson Center, "Research Programs: Future of Peace Operations Program."

49. Harvard University, John F. Kennedy School of Government, The Carr Center for Human Rights Policy, "National Security and Human Rights Program."

50. United States Holocaust Memorial Museum. "Responding to Threats of Genocide Today."

Case Study 1

American Intervention in Africa

Building on the Lessons of Somalia

Lt Col Aaron Steffens, USAF

Before images of starving refugees began to appear on their television screens in 1992, most Americans had never heard of Somalia—a small, arid country in the Horn of Africa. Although it installed a parliamentary democracy after gaining independence from Italy and Great Britain in 1960, Somalia was ruled from 1969 to 1991 by a corrupt dictator named Siad Barre, who seized power in a military coup. By the summer of 1992, the nation had become a failed state embroiled in a bitter civil war. With no police, no banking system, no functioning schools or hospitals, and no government, Somalia descended into chaos. Thousands of Somalis were dying every day from starvation, sickness, and violence that some were calling genocide.[1]

The international intervention that followed has become synonymous with a single event—the Battle of Mogadishu on 3 October 1993. On closer inspection, however, the challenges of what was actually a three-year operation have a great deal to offer the US military, especially in the broader context of Africa and the global war on terror. The US *National Security Strategy* lists three factors that enable terrorist networks to embed in failed and failing states—poverty, weak institutions, and corruption—and all of these are particularly virulent in Africa.[2]

Although the American experience in Somalia occurred in its own peculiar context, it holds valuable lessons for future operations in Africa, particularly in the light of present nation-building efforts in Iraq and Afghanistan. At the strategic level, Somalia illustrates the importance of prevention over intervention, the criticality of timing, and the abilities and inherent weaknesses of the United Nations. Operationally, it offers a clear warning to those who would intervene in weak and failing states—if the desired end state is long-term stability, there are no shortcuts. A lasting resolution necessitates political reconstruction, disarmament, unified effort, and a commitment to potential combat operations. Furthermore, achieving these objectives in the context of a politically viable intervention in Africa will require a radical shift in the US regional command structure and the ways in which American forces interact with African coalition partners and organizations.

Background

Although the violence and killing that precipitated international intervention has been termed genocide, the word fits uneasily in the context of the Somali situation. The United Nations Genocide Convention of 1948 defined genocide as the annihilation of not just national, but ethnic, racial, and religious groups.[3] Native Somalis, however, belong to a single racial and ethnic group, and they share a common religious and cultural tradition.[4] *Mass killing*, defined as the intentional killing of a massive number of noncombatants, is a more appropriate term for the violence, starvation, and death that wracked Somalia in the long period leading up to intervention.[5]

The regime of Siad Barre not only began the mass killings of Somali noncombatants, but in many ways it laid the catastrophic foundation for the cycle of brutality that would escalate once the regime itself imploded. Fueled by pan-Somali nationalism, Somalia invaded Ethiopia in 1977 in a bid to reclaim the Ogaden region, home to the ethnically Somali Ogadeni tribe. A bitter defeat by the Ethiopians, however, began the unraveling of Somali national unity and led to the first coup against Barre.[6] In retaliation, the Red Berets, members of Barre's personal bodyguard, massacred over 2,000 noncombatants, including women and children; their only crime was clan affiliation with an army officer involved in the coup.[7]

The disastrous Ogaden war unleashed a number of forces that eventually led to civil war. Most importantly for Siad Barre, the Ogadeni clan formed the bulk of Somali military leadership; when Barre renounced Somali claims to the Ogaden, he betrayed the group that had largely kept him in power since 1969.[8] As disaffection with Barre's regime continued to grow, government repression, and the mass killings it spawned, grew at a similar rate.

The Isaaq clan and its political element, the Somali National Movement (SNM), suffered a particularly compelling fate. After the SNM launched a military campaign in 1988 that occupied the cities of Burao and Hargeysa, government forces bombarded and destroyed both cities. From May to December of 1988, savage reprisals against the remaining Isaaq resulted in over 5,000 noncombatant deaths.[9] In addition, large numbers of the 300,000 Isaaq refugees who attempted to flee to Ethiopia were robbed and executed by regime forces; many were even strafed by the Somali Air Force. Africa Watch estimates that the Somali government killed over 50,000 Isaaq noncombatants from June 1988 to January 1990.[10]

At the same time, Siad Barre's grip on power was slipping fast. Torture and executions wracked the capital city of Mogadishu and its surroundings during his final days. Red Berets slaughtered 450 religious demonstrators on 14 July 1989. The next day, 47 primarily Isaaq civilians were executed en masse at a beach west of the city, and 65 noncombatants were gunned down on 6 July 1990 by Red Berets at a soccer stadium.[11] Siad Barre and his supporters finally fled Mogadishu in January 1991, ousted by a temporary coalition of insurgent groups led by the United Somali Congress (USC). Unfortunately for Somalia, the only common objective of the many insurgent factions was Barre's overthrow. All the groups were organized along clan lines with vague and shifting political and ideological manifestos. Inherently unstable, each faction began to unravel and vie for supremacy as soon as the dictator fled.[12]

In fact, the USC itself splintered almost immediately into two sides—that of Mohamed Farah Aideed, the USC's main military commander, who controlled the Habr Gedir subclan, and that of Ali Mahdi Mohamed, a wealthy Mogadishu hotelier and self-proclaimed interim president of Somalia, who controlled the Abgal subclan. Neither side showed any restraint in targeting civilians of the opposite clan. Africa Watch estimates that in Mogadishu alone, 14,000 people were killed and 27,000 wounded between 17 November 1991 and 29 February 1992.[13] The US-based Somali Community of the Americas, an admittedly anti-USC peace-advocacy group, reports that USC death squads executed hundreds of prominent intellectuals, businessmen, elders, and community leaders.[14]

Southern Somalia witnessed a brutal series of sweeps and occupations, first by Barre's retreating forces, then by Aideed-led USC forces, and finally by the Somali National Front (SNF). Each faction looted food stored in underground silos, stole or killed livestock, ruined wells, raped women of various clans, and killed men of opposing clans to prevent them from taking up arms.[15] These southern areas encompassed Somalia's richest farmlands, and the disruption caused by civil war, coupled with an intense drought, spurred a famine of epic proportions. By mid-1992, nearly all children in rural areas were reportedly suffering from malnutrition, and the death toll from starvation was estimated at 400,000 for the year.[16]

While many factors, including environmental ones, shaped the Somali famine, the specter of intentional mass killing was omnipresent. Control of food became the key to power and profit, and internationally donated aid was stolen, extorted, and hoarded by warring factions.[17] In fact, Africa Watch claims that the atrocities of the civil war and the use of food denial as a weapon were far more responsible for the massive starvation than the drought.[18]

Motivation

The segmented clan system at the heart of Somali society is critical to understanding the mass killing that wracked the country for many years. Although traditional Somali institutions and customary authorities had always existed outside the clan system, occupying colonial powers began discarding these in the first half of the twentieth century, and Siad Barre and Somali nationalists continued the task in the second half. This was a prerequisite for the forced adaptation of a nomadic, pastoral society to the strictures of a centralized, authoritarian state ruled by a small, elite class; in this context, system failure seemed almost assured. As the state crumbled and economic crises deepened, Somalis were forced to seek support on the basis of generalized kinship—they pursued clan interests without restraint and at the expense of all else.[19]

Mass killings, even the majority of those perpetrated by elements of Siad Barre's regime, fell out along clan lines. Motivations among both leaders and their executioners were complex—personal ambitions, clan rivalry, and a struggle for political power all played a role.[20] In addition, the competition for natural resources, such as productive farmland, dry-season pastures, and fuel reserve was significant. Ample evidence suggests that the long-term land resource objectives of many clans may have contributed substantially to the violence.[21]

Early Opportunities Missed

As national catastrophes like this one develop, mediation, conflict resolution, and other diplomatic measures should be the first line of attack.[22] Resort to military intervention in such a situation is like calling the fire department after the house is burning, the stove had been left on, smoke detectors were ignored, and household fire extinguishers were left unused. Accordingly, Mohamed Sahnoun, a well-regarded Algerian diplomat, has identified three specific instances representing classic crisis situations where the United Nations, and by extension the United States, might have intervened nonmilitarily without the expense and danger of calling the fire department.[23] Sahnoun, deputy director of the Organization of African Unity (OAU) and later a special representative to Somalia for the United Nations, watched the Somali situation unfold firsthand.[24]

The first opportunity to intervene was the brutal suppression of Somali noncombatants by government security forces as the civil war unfolded in the late 1980s. These atrocities, and all that would follow, did not happen in a vacuum. Two human rights organizations, Amnesty International and Africa Watch, documented and denounced the mass killings as they proliferated.[25] Interestingly, the US Department of State (DOS) and the US General Accounting Office published two of the most damning reports on the mass killings in 1989.[26] Although the United States took modest steps—the suspension of military aid and the freezing of economic support funds—the international community at large, and most conspicuously the United Nations, failed to react.[27]

The next opportunity happened in May 1990 after more than two years of civil war. A group of 144 prominent Somali intellectuals, business people, and tradesmen published a manifesto calling for the abolition of repressive laws, a multiparty political system, and a national reconciliation conference to end the civil war and prepare for national elections.[28] Siad Barre's reaction to the manifesto included arrests, contrived trials, and death sentences for 46 of the petition's signatories.[29] Although several countries, including the United States, suggested peace conferences and lodged diplomatic protests, "neither the UN nor the regional organizations were providing any leadership for serious mediation efforts, and the fragile and isolated endeavors of a few governments could have no impact."[30]

Sahnoun suggests that the final opportunity appeared just after Siad Barre and his security forces fled Mogadishu. At that point, the rival forces of Ali Mahdi Mohamed and Mohamed Farah Aideed maintained a precarious cease-fire in the capital city. The government of Djibouti took the opportunity to sponsor a reconciliation conference to promote peace and forge a stable government for Somalia. Neither regional organizations nor the United Nations, whose staff had completely evacuated Somalia at that point, participated. Although a number of issues hampered the conference, Sahnoun claims it was a lack of both UN leadership and international pressure that led the way to failure.[31]

Whether the international community could have disrupted Somalia's agonizing descent into anarchy is not certain, but awareness of that descent and the mass killings it engendered is unquestionable. The broader lesson is obvious but often unheeded—prevention is more effective and less expensive than rehabilitation.[32] As the aforementioned opportunities came and went, James Woods, deputy assistant secretary of defense for African affairs during the crisis, recalls that Somalia was "still a third-tier issue in the Washington scheme of things." The strategic value of Somalia had vanished along with the Cold War, and the interagency policy, operational, and intelligence desks assigned to the country were understaffed and short on information.[33] Somaliland president Muhammad Ibrahim Egal, when questioned in 1997 about the reluctance of the international community to investigate recently unearthed mass graves, summed up the Somali point of view. "I have now come to the conclusion that when this genocide was being executed . . . the international community watched with apathy. Nobody moved a finger to even object or condemn, let alone stop it. So, I think it is a sort of guilty conscience."[34]

International Intervention: UN Operations in Somalia (UNOSOM)

Boutros Boutros-Ghali, the first UN secretary-general of the post–Cold War period, took the helm in January 1992 with a mandate for aggressive leadership. He envisioned a new role for the United Nations as the world's principle peacemaker and peace enforcer.[35] Coincident with Boutros-Ghali's inauguration, Aideed and Ali Mahdi began the wholesale slaughter of noncombatants in Mogadishu with heavy artillery, finally piquing significant UN interest in Somalia. After several UN-brokered cease-fires of varying success, UNSCR 751 passed in April 1992, establishing the UN Operation in Somalia (UNOSOM) with 50 UN observers, as well as provisions for more, under the direction of Mohamed Sahnoun.[36]

Sahnoun confronted a peacekeeper's nightmare—grasping warlords, no government with which to negotiate, and a mounting humanitarian crisis. In particular, Aideed, deeply suspicious of the United Nations, remained in a continual power struggle with Ali Mahdi, whom Aideed felt was the object of UN favoritism. With increasing intransigence, Aideed succeeded in limiting UNOSOM in size, function, and, eventually, effectiveness.[37] The UN leadership in New York facilitated Aideed's success by focusing attentions solely on the Aideed–Ali Mahdi struggle, ignoring the hundreds of other Somali elders and leaders with whom Mohamed Sahnoun had successful dealings.[38]

In addition, Sahnoun was undercut by the inability of agencies such as the UN High Commission on Refugees (UNHCR) and the UN World Food Program (UNWFP) to organize successful aid distribution systems, to coordinate their efforts with each other, and to deal with UNOSOM.[39] The final straw was a currency and weapons delivery to Ali Mahdi by a Russian aircraft with UN markings chartered by the UNWFP. UN leadership in New York was unwilling or unable to explain the debacle. Frustrated with UN bureaucracy, Mohamed Sahnoun resigned in October 1992, and UNOSOM soon ceased to be an effective force.[40]

Any analysis of UNOSOM's accomplishments must be viewed in the context of its mandate—it was conceived and organized under UN Charter chapter 6 as a small, traditional peacekeeping operation to separate warring Somali parties and facilitate aid distribution.[41] Indeed, by October 1992, UNOSOM's efforts had resulted in a halt to fighting in Somalia outside Mogadishu and an anticipated Horn-of-Africa peace conference (actually held in 1993 in Addis Ababa, Ethiopia). On the other hand, UN missteps and Aideed's propaganda had combined to make the United Nations an enemy to much of the Somali population, especially in volatile Mogadishu, further hampering the efforts of all relief organizations.[42] So much so, that by November, all Mogadishu factions were shelling UN encampments and ships, looting warehouses, and obstructing aid convoys. Consequently, Boutros Boutros-Ghali recognized the need for a radical change in the UN Security Council's mandate towards Somalia.[43]

American Involvement

As UNOSOM formed during the spring of 1992, the US government vacillated over the unfolding crisis. Although institutionalized checks and balances make the process slow, unwieldy, and often frustrating, there are common issues that generally drive democracies toward intervention. These include large refugee flows to developed states, the media spotlight on humanitarian suffering, continued defiance by unseemly rulers, and ineffective sanctions. In combination with the relative size and power of the country concerned and the likelihood of a successful outcome, all these factors coalesce into an imperative Karin von Hippel called the "Do Something" effect.[44]

By July 1992, the pressure on the Bush administration from Congress, aid agencies, and the public to do something about Somalia was intense.[45] Concurrently, interest and involvement with the situation at the staff level, in the DOS, the Office of the Secretary of Defense (OSD), the Joint Staff (JS), and the National Security Council (NSC), had also increased dramatically.[46] A flurry of interagency discussion, building on previous planning, produced four options for the president's consideration: flooding Somalia with air-dropped food aid; auctioning high-value food at low prices to Somali merchants; deploying US troops to strengthen UN peacekeeping forces already in place; and armed US intervention to establish a safe haven in southern Somalia.[47]

Airpower Intervention: Operation Provide Relief

On 13 August, the president chose a variation on the first option, and by 18 August, US Central Command (CENTCOM) had formed Joint Task Force-Operation Provide Relief (JTF-OPR). JTF-OPR's stated mission was the immediate airlift of food aid to Somalia and refugee camps in Kenya and the transport of personnel and equipment for additional UN security forces.[48] Ten US Air Force (USAF) C-130 aircraft and 400 personnel were deployed to Mombasa, Kenya, 150 miles south of the Somali border, to begin air transport operations to UN and nongovernmental organization (NGO) agencies in the isolated interior.[49] Along with Belgian, German, and Canadian military aircraft, USAF assets delivered 28,000 metric tons of critical supplies, some air-dropped, to isolated dirt airstrips in the most devastated areas of Somalia.[50]

JTF-OPR continued operations through February 1993, flying a total of 2,500 sorties. Overall, it succeeded admirably in providing an immediate response to the "Do Something" effect; extensive media images scored a public relations coup for the Bush administration, with minimal risk to US forces.[51] The long-term results, however, are mired in controversy. Air Mobility Command (AMC), citing summary reports by two NGOs, claims that JTF-OPR played a crucial role in breaking the Somali famine.[52] Other sources, including the International Committee of the Red Cross (ICRC), conclude that the operation "had little impact on the famine and no impact on the continued banditry, extortion, and clan warfare that made emergency food delivery problematic."[53] Although true to a large extent, this argument misses the broader point. Only airpower has the ability to deliver large quantities of aid at a moment's notice into semihostile territory with almost no political repercussions. Time is critical in humanitarian assistance operations, and involvement on the ground with the politics of food distribution would have meant a significant increase in risk and a corresponding delay in initiation.[54]

An Unprecedented Effort: Operation Restore Hope

As UNOSOM was overcome by events in Somalia, November 1992 brought an unprecedented opinion shift to the Washington interagency debate on intervention. Although CENTCOM leadership and the Joint Chiefs of Staff (JCS) had previously opposed intervention based on concerns about unclear objectives and a wishful exit strategy, planning at the JS J-3/Operations and J-5/Plans and Policy levels had continued throughout the fall.[55] By November, the Deputies' Committee of the NSC was facing intense political pressure—fighting had closed all Somali seaports, looting of airlifted food was rampant, UNOSOM was unable to venture outside its defensive compound, and the death toll continued to climb. In addition, the committee felt a growing interagency consensus that "US interests in global stability would be well served by a muscular UN peace enforcement capability to manage growing regional crises."[56] Once the JCS chairman, Gen Colin Powell, consented to intervention, momentum and consensus built rapidly within the NSC Deputies Committee, and three policy options were presented to the president on 25 November.[57]

The first option was risk averse and minimalist, calling for logistical support, protection, and firepower in support of an expanded contingent of 3,500 UN peacekeepers. No American troops would deploy on the ground in Somalia, but US airpower and sea power would be readily available to the UN forces. The second option, termed the "ball-peen hammer" option, involved 5,000 US ground troops to secure the Somali seaports, airports, and main lines of communication in order to enable relief convoys into the famine zones. This plan included an extensive diplomatic component to ensure the cooperation of the various warlords, and it was the preferred interagency course of action. Finally, the "sledgehammer" option envisioned a full-scale, decisive intervention—15,000 troops with the required logistics support for engineering, civil affairs, and reconstruction projects.[58]

Perhaps spurred by General Powell's predilection for overwhelming force, Pres. George H. W. Bush, now a lame-duck politician, surprised most of his advisors by reaching for the "sledgehammer." The administration quickly closed ranks, however; within 24 hours, Gen Joseph P. Hoar, CENTCOM commander, even received approval to double the troop contingent to 30,000. The public reasons for such a large-scale humanitarian intervention in the absence of a vital national interest were summarized by the president in an address to the American people—moral imperatives and a commitment to international stability required decisive action. Privately, a majority of government leadership sensed in Somalia an opportunity to "establish a foreign policy precedent on the cheap." With the deployment of overwhelming force, Somalia became low-risk, at least in theory, and it presented the opportunity to debut an unprecedented program of assertive multilateralism tailored to the destabilizing small wars and collapsing states of the post–Cold War era.[59]

Boutros Boutros-Ghali initially greeted the US contribution, expected to cost $450 million, as an answer to the United Nations' problems in Somalia; although he had originally pushed for overall UN command of any operation, he quickly acquiesced to the US-led Unified Task Force (UNITAF). Organized under UN Charter chapter 7 as a peace-enforcement mission, UNITAF ostensibly had three functions: to secure Somalia's main ports, airfields, and regional transport hubs; to open supply routes and secure feeding centers; and to create a secure environment for handoff to UNOSOM II, the follow-up to the UN Operation in Somalia mission.[60] Building on the president's strategic guidance, CENTCOM took great pains to sharply limit the scope of the operation.[61] The civil-affairs and military-police training components that were part of the original policy concept were removed. In addition, the first drafts of UNSCR 794, which authorized UNITAF, were written in the Pentagon specifically to satisfy CENTCOM concerns about mission creep towards any semblance of nation building.[62]

A total of 37,000 multinational troops, anchored by 24,000 US marines and soldiers, deployed for Operation Restore Hope under the command of Marine lieutenant general Robert B. Johnston beginning on 9 December. Two days prior, Robert Oakley, US special envoy to Somalia, had succeeded in forcing Aideed and Ali Mahdi into a temporary cease-fire for the duration of UNITAF's mission. US diplomatic power, backed by tremendous military force, even compelled the two bitter warlords to shake hands for the media.[63] Within a few weeks and with minimal casualties, UNITAF had opened ports, airfields, and highways; major cities in its area of operations were occupied and secure; and the famine and indirect mass killing of Somalis was stopped. In fact, Lieutenant General Johnston informed Washington in late January that "the war's over, we won, it's time to come home."[64] Although limited redeployments had begun by 20 January 1993, UN concern about a host of issues, including militia disarmament, kept UNITAF forces in Somalia until 4 May.[65]

Indeed, Boutros-Ghali and the United Nations were deeply concerned about self-imposed limits on UNITAF's Operation Restore Hope mandate from the beginning of the operation. On 8 December, the secretary-general wrote President Bush about the necessity of disarming irregular troops, establishing a secure environment outside of UNITAF's designated area of operations, and ensuring that compatible political and humanitarian conditions were in place and maintained during the transfer to UNOSOM II.[66] Key US political leaders, however, were often contradictory in their policy statements and directives, especially concerning the critical issue of disarmament.[67] Thus, Johnston and Oakley, as the military and diplomatic leaders in-theater, had substantial authority to interpret policy as they saw fit—a result that had heavy implications for UNOSOM II.[68]

As seen through a strict construction lens—a short-term, limited mission focused only on humanitarian relief—Operation Restore Hope was a rousing success. Although UNITAF was not required to rebuild infrastructure, many roads and bridges were repaired; although it had no mandate for disarmament, some small arms and heavy weapons were seized; and although it was not directed to organize local forces, a substantial number of personnel was recruited and employed as police for local security operations.[69] Critics charge that the failure to completely disarm the militias, which only UNITAF had the coercive power to attempt, and the failure to establish basic social and political structures doomed the smaller, weaker, and less well-organized UNOSOM II to failure.[70] In hindsight, these charges may be accurate, but they speak to a much broader critique of US and UN intervention policy—Johnston and UNITAF had fulfilled their missions, albeit narrowly interpreted, quickly and effectively.

Failure and Withdrawal: UNOSOM II

Although UNSCR 814 structured UNOSOM II as a chapter 7 peace-enforcement operation, just like UNITAF, that is where any similarity ended. UNOSOM II was free to use "all necessary means" to carry out an historically broad mandate—the resurrection of a failed state—from disarmament to nation building. To accomplish this daunting task, Turkish general Cevik Bir, the military commander, and Adm Jonathan Howe, the secretary-general's special representative, had less than 26,000 troops by September 1993, versus the 37,000 that deployed for UNITAF. In addition, they lacked sufficient numbers of armored vehicles and helicopters, many of their troops were poorly trained and ill equipped, and the majority of their forces deferred to home-country instructions before following UN commands. US forces dwindled to 2,900 logistics support personnel and a quick-reaction force of 1,100 troops offshore.[71]

Not surprisingly, the Somali warlords, who had lain low for UNITAF's five-month tenure, began to reassert themselves almost immediately on UNOSOM II's arrival. In particular, UN forces and Mohamed Aideed, who maintained an almost paranoid fear of marginalization, spent the month of May locked in a cycle of mutual antagonism.[72] The posturing turned deadly on 5 June, when 24 virtually defenseless Pakistani soldiers were killed after their comrades performed an ill-advised and ill-coordinated weapons inspection at a radio station controlled by the Somali National Alliance (SNA), Aideed's primary military arm. Outraged and fearing a worldwide loss of credibility, with the complete support of the US government, the United Nations acted quickly. UNSCR 837, calling for the arrest and punishment of those responsible, effectively created a state of war between Aideed's forces and UNOSOM II and, by extension, the United States.[73]

The war lasted four months and overturned the solid reconciliatory progress that had been made to that point. Somali culture requires a temporary end to hostilities, and sometimes even cooperation, between warring clans in the face of foreign threats, and the fight with Aideed began to systematically erode popular support for the United Nations.[74] The turning point was a 12 July attack on an alleged SNA command center by US AH-1 Cobra attack helicopters that killed up to 70 traditional clan leaders and civilians, most of them unassociated with Aideed. The attack turned popular sentiment solidly against the UN intervention, and even USC forces loyal to Ali Mahdi began to display open contempt for UNOSOM II.[75]

In August Pres. Bill Clinton acquiesced to General Howe's request for 400 additional US Army Special Forces soldiers, a group called Task Force Ranger. Although General Powell and Secretary of Defense Les Aspin were initially opposed to the escalation, they relented after an improvised explosive device killed four American soldiers. Still, Aspin refused a corollary request for additional armor and airpower assets, based on his desire to limit militarization and pursue a "coordinated economic-political-security approach."[76]

Aspin was far from the only critic of UNOSOM II's military obsession with Aideed. As repeated attempts to capture or kill the warlord failed and civilian casualties mounted, members of Congress, humanitarian NGOs, regional organizations, and even key UNOSOM II participants like Italy and France, all proclaimed the derailment of the United Nations' economic and political rehabilitation mission by military preoccupations.[77] Meanwhile, the US interagency community, led by Clinton's new NSC Deputies Committee, was virtually schizophrenic in its pursuit of dueling agendas. Tremendous capital was expended in persuading and assisting the United Nations to fulfill its broad nation-building mandate. Simultaneously, and contrary to later assertions, the United States was "deeply and enthusiastically" engaged in the military confrontation with Aideed.[78]

That military confrontation climaxed on 3 October in the Battle of Mogadishu, with 18 US servicemen killed and 78 wounded. Notably, the United Nations had few connections to

Task Force Ranger; its commander reported directly to CENT-COM, and US National Command Authority specifically approved each mission. President Clinton, hounded by congressional and public criticism, adopted a new policy focused on force protection while seeking a quick withdrawal under "circumstances other than humiliation."[79] This sent other countries scrambling for the exits and effectively ended the United Nations' practical ability to succeed in its operation. All US forces withdrew by 31 March 1994, while UNOSOM II lingered for almost a year, accomplishing little, until its mandate expired in March 1995.[80]

Strategic Lessons

They didn't stop any fighting, they didn't build the country. No water in Mogadishu, no electricity, no roads, rubbish everywhere, and they spent billions of dollars. What did they do with it? Instead of building things, they destroyed.

Mogadishu resident, March 1994

The popular American perception of the Somali operation—as a series of UN missteps capped by a US military catastrophe—is incomplete and misleading. While the reality is much more complex, Somalia's current situation is indicative of the overall effectiveness of multinational efforts at change from 1991 to 1995. The country remains an international basket case without an effective national government or significant prospects for reform. It is dominated by the petty interests of warlords, plagued by fits of violence, and hobbled by a never-ending series of humanitarian crises. Even worse from the US perspective, Somalia has the potential to become another focal point in the global war on terrorism. In May 2005, Maj Gen Sam Helland, commander of Combined Joint Task Force–Horn of Africa (CJTF-HOA), noted that Somalia is "ungoverned space," and it has become a safe haven for terrorists in East Africa.[81]

Despite the glaring failure of the overall intervention, each of the distinct Somali operations brought limited successes and generated important lessons for future missions that are often overshadowed by the Battle of Mogadishu. Reactions to the battle itself were swift—less than seven months later, in April 1994, the Clinton administration refused to respond to the horrific genocide in Rwanda. That same month the president issued Presidential Decision Directive 25 (PDD-25), a document that sharply curtailed the future of US armed humanitarian intervention and constituted a sea change from the assertive multilateralism adopted by the administration at its inauguration.[82]

The initiation of the global war on terror, however, portends a new era with increased stakes for operations like those conducted in Somalia—now defined in joint doctrine as complex contingency operations.[83] In fact, the US National Defense Strategy points specifically to the reorientation of military capabilities to confront the "irregular challenges" exposed by US experience in the war on terrorism. Many of those challenges are posed by an absence of effective government in nations like Somalia that creates sanctuaries for terrorists, criminals, and insurgents.[84] The ambitious command philosophy of CJTF-HOA, the American military organization now responsible for Somalia, is particularly instructive. It seeks to set the conditions for economic growth, spur education and prosperity, and provide a stable, secure environment for all the nations in its region.[85] Thus, the interventionism currently inherent in US foreign policy highlights both a propensity towards future complex contingency operations and the need to correctly interpret and incorporate the many lessons of Somalia.

Prevention

The first lesson is often cited but seldom heeded. The massive cost of Operation Restore Hope, about $1.97 billion, was six times greater than the total development assistance dedicated to Somalia for the previous three decades; an ounce of prevention is literally worth a pound of cure. Democracies are driven largely by short-term political expediencies, and thus they are prone to "magnify the benefits of avoiding immediate expenditures and discount the disadvantages of incurring future ones."[86] As previously mentioned, there were at least three clear opportunities prior to the formation of UNOSOM I where US leadership and UN involvement might have mitigated the Somali crisis.

Although initial efforts will normally employ instruments of national power other than the military, regional combatant commanders' resources and manpower may give them an advantage in identifying potential crises early. Commanders should be motivated by self-interest to drive the interagency process towards engagement short of intervention. In addition, the use of theater security cooperation plans to synchronize and integrate peacetime military activities on a regional basis should make regional combatant commands much more vocal advocates of prevention strategies.[87]

Timing

If prevention should fail and military intervention is contemplated, timing becomes a critical issue in the planning, execution, and exit strategy of any operation. In humanitarian crises, especially those akin to Somalia where the aim is to halt mass killing, earlier action is always better. In that context, intervention should be viewed as a process—the airlift of Operation Provide Relief began saving lives in August 1993, four full months before political considerations permitted UNITAF to land in Mogadishu.

Another important aspect of timing is the danger of time limits. In general, publicized limits indicate that important criteria, like national interest, moral imperative, and public support, have not been met.[88] Although President Bush's announcement that UNITAF would depart Somalia by the end of his term in office played well to Congress, the military, and the American public, it had dire consequences for the mission as a whole. Mohamed Aideed pacified his militia and welcomed US troops, whom he knew would soon leave, while simultaneously vilifying the United Nations in preparation for his coming confrontation with UNOSOM II.[89]

In addition, reconciliation amongst Somalis was impossible. Those elements of society amenable to negotiation, those who did not derive power from the barrel of a gun, were unable to reappear and coalesce in such a short time frame. Somalia's slide into anarchy took many years, and any meaningful attempt at state restoration would take a comparable amount of time.[90]

Relationships with the United Nations

After the Battle of Mogadishu, the Clinton administration worked overtime to apportion blame to the United Nations. Despite this, the organization remains an indispensable partner; America needs the United Nations as its proxy, its collaborator, and its mantle of legitimacy.[91] As the handoff from UNITAF to UNOSOM II illustrated, however, the United Nations is an inherently weak organization, both by design and by virtue of the budgetary and political constraints imposed by member states.[92] It was not designed to take over a task as daunting as Somalia. Therefore, it is not clear that perfect policy making and maximum efficiency, which were certainly not the case for UNOSOM II, would have enabled successful reconciliation.[93]

Of course, this was not recognized at the time. Although the sharply limited mandate of UNITAF contributed markedly to the failure of UNOSOM II, the Clinton administration was frenetic in its attempts to prove the United Nations capable.[94] Instead, the lesson of Somalia is one of responsibility. In any UN operation involving the United States, American forces should not only expect to shoulder a majority of the burden, they should willingly take on the leadership responsibility if they expect to succeed.[95]

Operational Lessons

The stark contrast between the success of UNITAF and the apparent failure of UNOSOM II highlights both a dilemma at the heart of complex contingency operations and a critical lesson that straddles the line between strategic and operational contexts. The dilemma involves an alleged distinction between purely humanitarian intervention, symbolized by the efficient triumph of UNITAF, and nation building, symbolized by the disaster of UNOSOM II. Is it possible to separate the two? In Somalia's particular context, experience suggests that any attempt to do so—to apply a humanitarian Band–Aid without addressing the underlying political issues—is doomed to failure.[96]

Political Reconstruction

The root causes of the mass killing, the civil war, and even the famine that gripped Somalia were political in nature. US leaders were loath to acknowledge this because it implied a more difficult and risky mission of uncertain length. Instead, UNITAF provided a semblance of order for a short time, and then it ducked the difficult political questions that flowed from the decision to intervene and quickly left. Furthermore, the notion that any similar operation could remain above significant political interference is flawed—landing 37,000 foreign troops in a failed state inherently and drastically impacts that domestic political scene, especially when those troops begin to create order and stability where none existed before.[97]

Deputy Assistant Secretary of Defense James Woods, the chairman of the Somalia Task Force in the OSD during the operation, has concluded that there were three main flaws in US policy with respect to the operation as a whole. First, US forces deployed only to restore security, not to decide a political outcome; second, the United States would not disarm warlords and gangs; and last, the United Nations was left to attempt to revitalize the minimal elements of a functioning Somali society and government, a task that it was incapable of accomplishing.[98] Complex contingency operations, especially those labeled peace-enforcement operations under UN chapter 7, are usually "political operations carried out by military means." Therefore, humanitarian relief, rebuilding infrastructure, implementing political functions, restoring government institutions, demobilization, and reintegrating militias and armies are central to the success of these missions.[99] In fact, joint doctrine now emphasizes the importance of a political-military plan that addresses these exact issues. As current operations in Iraq and Afghanistan suggest, eliminating terrorist havens dictates that successful intervention end states focus on political stability and restored security.[100]

Disarmament

The functional task of demobilization and disarmament offers a clear lesson on the necessity for conflict resolution in planning for end states. It also highlights the largest chasm that erupted between UNITAF and UNOSOM II in Somalia operations. All Somali factions had agreed to disarm in the March 1993 Addis Ababa accords; in fact, many Somalis that expected disarmament were surprised by UNITAF's lack of action.[101] The warlords quickly realized that the United States was not serious about challenging their power, and there would be essentially no changes to the military situation on the ground. This meant two things: that the warlords could wait out UNITAF and then challenge UN troops who they knew to be much less formidable, and that the security situation in Somalia would remain chaotic. In simplified form, security is the first step in reconciliation, which leads to conflict resolution, which is a vital part of creating a stable end state.[102]

The question of disarmament also reveals a fundamental divide between academics, who stress disarmament's necessity, and warriors, who stress its inherent complications. Most scholars argue correctly that with the proper mandate and its initial momentum, UNITAF could have removed most of the heavy weapons from factional militias with minimal conflict.[103] But this line of reasoning ignores two major complications. First, the building of political and civic institutions must proceed concurrently in order to replace the security that arms provide.[104] Second, "if the disarmament of the population becomes an objective, then there should be no mistaking the fact that the troops given this mission have been committed to combat."[105] Disarmament, then, is not incompatible with complex contingency operations; it simply necessitates the organization, training, and equipment that combat operations require. Unfortunately, UNOSOM II came up short of that standard, resembling a peacekeeping force far more than it did a combat force.

Legitimacy and Impartiality

Another issue that arises in a failed state like Somalia is the question of legitimacy. Since legally sanctioned authorities and state structures are nonexistent, should the United States deal with, and thereby confer legitimacy upon, whoever has more men, more guns, and a better media apparatus? Those actions in Somalia led UNITAF into one-sided relationships with warlords who not only lacked any political authority bestowed by the Somali people, but whose crimes against those same people were well known.[106] The various warlords thrived financially in the absence of a government, so they had no desire to see one built; instead, they attempted to manipulate unwitting intervention forces, often successfully, into boosting their own power bases and neutralizing their enemies.[107]

Viable reconciliation in Somalia necessitated a drastic change in the balance of power away from those who advocated and sustained violence, mainly the warlords and their supporters, and towards those who sought peace. Such an effort would have required both time and a willingness to take sides, because making peace means deciding who rules. Although politicians often favor an impartial middle course like that chosen in Somalia, it is usually counterproductive. The deployment of an overwhelming, combat-ready force should enable an intervening coalition to install a leader of its choosing until national self-determination is viable. The necessity of developing such a long-term political plan prior to the commencement of operations, along with the means to enforce it, is one of UNITAF's most enduring lessons.[108]

Unified Effort

The US joint after-action report on Operation Restore Hope notes that, "with the benefit of hindsight, it is possible to see that operations in Somalia were successful when they recognized the trinity of diplomatic, military, and humanitarian actions—and remarkably less so when they did not."[109] For instance, civil affairs units were sorely lacking in UNITAF, although planning dictated 300 civil affairs personnel, the JCS opposed activating reservists for an anticipated six-week operation, and so only 36 personnel were deployed. In addition, development aid and expertise for anything other than feeding Somalis was insufficient throughout the operation. In an effort to disassociate itself from nation building, UNITAF often avoided or excluded government agencies and NGOs with the practical political or economic competencies that a failed state like Somalia required.[110] The daunting quest for a stable and legitimate end state, however, must necessarily harness the expertise and resources of every organization willing to contribute.

The most critical organizations in Somalia were humanitarian NGOs. After all, their success in feeding starving Somalis was UNITAF's raison d'etre. Col Kevin Kennedy, the commander of the Civil Military Operations Center (CMOC) during UNITAF, notes several lessons from the military/humanitarian NGO relationship. First, there was "no contact at the operational level" between CENTCOM planners and humanitarian NGOs during the planning phase of the operation.[111] In addition, different interpretations of the UNITAF mission led to different levels of military support for NGOs and the frustration that comes with unfulfilled expectations. Finally, the security environment that UNITAF established did not include police functions by design, and NGOs frequently saw this as a failure to support humanitarian operations.[112]

Joint doctrine now dictates the development of campaign plans to leverage the core competencies of all government agencies and NGOs toward a common set of objectives.[113] Although priorities, command arrangements, and operating principles will certainly vary amongst both international and domestic military and nonmilitary participants, US joint force commanders should view themselves as coordinators and consensus builders. The US military is likely to play a supporting, rather than supported, role in complex contingency operations, and only a top-down emphasis on unified effort from the beginning stages of planning will leverage the strengths of all participants.[114]

Airpower

Another important operational lesson from Somalia is the critical, and sometimes controversial, role of airpower. Airlift was essential to the overall effort in deploying and sustaining the initial ground forces. During the first six weeks of the mission, AMC aircraft delivered 24,500 tons of cargo and approximately 24,000 passengers to Somalia. Perhaps even more important to future humanitarian operations, however, airlift provided the capability in the previous months during Operation Provide Hope to insert humanitarian aid quickly with few political repercussions.[115]

Other airpower missions, however, are more significant for their controversial effects in the Somali context, and they highlight issues that may not be immediately apparent to military professionals. Helicopters of all types, from the tiny AH-6 Little Birds to the ubiquitous MH–60s, provided critical insertion and reconnaissance capabilities throughout Mogadishu. Nevertheless, critics charge that the virtually constant presence of loud, low-flying US aircraft eventually aroused tremendous anger on behalf of the entire population, even those who initially welcomed foreign intervention. When this constant air presence was combined with a series of air strikes in June 1993, the result contributed substantially to the steady erosion of popular support for the United Nations.[116]

In addition, the same force issues that plagued the operation as a whole also trickled down into airpower employment. Strike aircraft were used as both a coercive and a blunt-force instrument against the warlords and their forces with mixed results. At the beginning of UNOSOM II, the mere presence of AC-130 gunships and AH-1 Cobra helicopters provided some deterrence to coerce the various clans to allow humanitarian assistance operations to proceed. In June 1993, AC-130s attacked several complexes belonging to Aideed and the SNA in an effort to force cooperation, and the results were generally successful.[117]

The infamous SNA command center attack of 12 July, however, crossed a line that was imperceptible to UNOSOM II but quite obvious to the citizens of Mogadishu. For Somalis, it signaled a departure from coercion to blunt-force attack, and it represented a declaration of war. Not only was most of Mogadishu turned against UNOSOM II, but the UN attempted to conduct the war without the necessary forces, equipment, or political resolve.[118]

African Intervention

A summary of Somalia's strategic and operational lessons highlights the notion that complex contingency operations should always begin with the promulgation of a desired end state. If that end state represents long-term stability, then the mission necessitates not only a comprehensive intervention focused on disarmament, reconciliation, and political restructuring, it also implies conflict and combat. Regardless of attempts to circumvent the oft-maligned task of nation building, it consistently reappears as the only long-term solution. Of course, this is precisely the task with which US forces in Iraq and Afghanistan are currently engaged.[119] Is this a model for the future?

The American experience in Somalia continues to affect US policy towards Africa today. For critics of peace operations, interventions, and the United Nations, the Battle of Mogadishu is a potent symbol of the difficulties and dangers inherent in African intervention. Simultaneously, current US policy is quick to recognize that the strategic situation in much of Africa poses a threat to a core value of the United States, preserving human dignity, and to a strategic priority, combating global terrorism. Since 1991 US forces have conducted 31 contingency operations in sub-Saharan Africa. In addition, America will import 25 percent of its oil from West Africa by 2015, surpassing the volume currently shipped from the Persian Gulf.[120] Thus, Africa remains locked in a peculiar paradox. It is likely to become the next focus in the global war on terrorism, but it is the continent where the United States is least engaged. Its need for complex contingency operations is greatest, but its hold on politicians and the American people is the least.

Accordingly, US contributions to future operations in Africa will probably be short on troops and long on overhead. Complex contingency operations dedicated to long-term success will require large contributions of regional manpower to complement American support, firepower, and intelligence capabilities. Although many African militaries are rich in peacekeeping experience and leadership talent, US planners must realize that few of them possess specialized units in addition to their basic needs, and many lack necessary skills and equipment. With the exception of South Africa, and to a lesser extent Ghana and Nigeria, none are capable of regional force projection or sustained, intense combat operations.[121] In particular, "militaries in sub-Saharan Africa are weak at maintenance of complex equipment, strategic mobility, advanced command, control, and intelligence, airpower, and naval power."[122] Fortunately, these are precisely the areas where the US military excels.

The African Standby Force (ASF) represents a unique opportunity for the United States to combine these capabilities with

African manpower to provide an intervention force that addresses many of the shortfalls of Operation Restore Hope. In July 2004, the African heads of state, under the aegis of the African Union (AU), approved the policy framework of the ASF. The concept envisions five regional standby brigades (3,000 to 4,000 troops), which will provide the AU with a combined standby capacity of 15,000 to 20,000 troops. The core of each brigade will reside in one of the five African regions and, in theory, be able to quickly organize, deploy, and intervene to stem early violence before it erupts into full-scale war.[123] The plan calls for each brigade to field four light infantry battalions with the requisite engineering, signals, reconnaissance, military police, logistics, and medical support units, as well as four helicopters and a variety of light to medium vehicles.[124]

The AU has designed its concept around six missions: military advisor missions, regional observer missions codeployed with the United Nations, stand-alone observer missions, chapter 6 regional peacekeeping missions, complex contingency peace operations, and genocide intervention missions. The military components of each mission are designed to deploy within 30 days of receiving an AU mandate, with the exception of genocide missions that deploy within 14 days. A unified effort is envisioned from the beginning of each operation, and the ASF also includes 240 civilian police and a roster of civilian experts to address human rights, humanitarian, governance, demobilization, disarmament, repatriation, and reconstruction issues.[125]

June 2005 was the target date for operational status on the first four missions above, and June 2010 is the target for the last two. Although substantive progress has occurred, the AU is struggling to overcome funding issues for a program that is extraordinarily ambitious by African standards. At the Group of Eight (G8) summit of 2003, leaders of the developed nations expressed strong support of the AU concept, but they failed to award specific funding based on concerns about the scope and cost of the framework, instead endorsing a scaled-down version of the original plan.[126] In 2004 the G8 pledged to train 50,000 African peacekeepers over the next five to six years, but details of this commitment are sketchy.[127]

US Involvement

The ASF represents a unique opportunity to facilitate African solutions to African problems at minimal expense. Although the AU is exploring a range of African funding initiatives, international donations of money, equipment, and expertise could easily pay for themselves many times over in years to come. The estimated 2004 three-year start-up costs for the ASF were approximately $17 million.[128] By way of comparison, this is the same amount that Operation Iraqi Freedom consumes every three hours based on 2004 US government figures.[129]

As part of the 2005 Global Peace Operations Initiative (GPOI), US European Command (EUCOM) is working with lead nations and regional organizations, particularly the Economic Community of West African States (ECOWAS), to support, equip, and train African forces. EUCOM also plans to expand exercise activity, under the aegis of the Africa Contingency Operations Training and Assistance Program, aimed at enhancing African capacity to conduct peace-support operations.[130] With more emphasis, funding, and vision, these efforts could be an excellent link between the US military and a future ASF.

Unfortunately, from its name to its headquarters and operating bases, EUCOM is clearly focused on Europe. In recognition of the escalating strategic value of African engagement, the United States should make a bold move—replacing the current tripartite regional combatant command structure for the continent with US Africa Command (US AFRICOM). AFRICOM could dramatically increase American engagement "in the region—analyzing intelligence, working closely with civil-military leaders, coordinating training, conducting exercises, and constantly planning for various contingencies."[131] The AU has already identified strategic airlift, early warning, limited technical and logistical capacities, and command and control as ASF capability shortfalls that require international assistance.[132] AFRICOM could address these with robust training and exercises, interoperability measures, and personnel exchange programs.*

---

*On 6 February 2007, Pres. G. W. Bush directed that Africa Command be established. The command began initial operations in October 2007, and at the time of publication was situated at Kelley Barracks, Stuttgart, Germany.

Perhaps a future African genocide or humanitarian crisis might be addressed with an African solution. Under a mandate from the AU, the ASF would deploy a regional standby brigade using US strategic airlift. AFRICOM would assist with logistics, communications, and command and control. RQ-1 Predators would provide intelligence, surveillance, and reconnaissance, while EC-130 Commando Solos implemented an ASF-designed psychological operations campaign. If necessary, AC-130s or similar strike platforms could carry out coercive or ground support missions directed by a trained ASF control party. By relying heavily on airpower and leveraging its military strengths, the United States could limit its personnel in the country of interest to the absolute minimum.

Facilitating such an African intervention capability addresses many of the lessons of Somalia. Strategically, a combination of multilateral African manpower and US assistance would likely engender UN support while simultaneously ensuring American leadership and avoiding reliance on UN capabilities. From a domestic political perspective, such an option would present little risk of US casualties, it could be implemented quickly, and it could proceed almost without time limits. Well-trained ASF troops, backed by US airpower, would have the moxie necessary to disarm adversaries.

Also, regional African forces, in addition to bearing a mantle of legitimacy, would possess the cultural, linguistic, and religious knowledge to successfully navigate complex operations. Most importantly, however, the next-door neighbor aspect of the ASF would compel it to address the political issues behind the crisis within the framework of a unified effort in order to forge a long-term, comprehensive solution. After all, Somalia remains a source of regional instability, destitute refugees, piracy, and organized crime almost 15 years after the international intervention, and no one knows that better than Somalia's neighbors.

Notes

1. Makinda, *Seeking Peace from Chaos*, 11–19.
2. The White House, *National Security Strategy of the United States*, 2002, 4.
3. Valentino, *Final Solutions*, 9.

4. Makinda, *Seeking Peace from Chaos*, 18.
5. Valentino, *Final Solutions*, 10.
6. Makinda, *Seeking Peace from Chaos*, 20.
7. Samatar, "Chapter 1: The Historical Setting: Somalia's Difficult Decade, 1980–1990, Persecution of the Majerteen."
8. Lewis, *Modern History of Somalia*, 156.
9. Samatar, "Chapter 1: The Historical Setting: Somalia's Difficult Decade, 1980–1990, Oppression of the Isaaq."
10. Ofcansky, "Chapter 5: National Security: Human Rights."
11. Samatar, "Chapter 1: The Historical Setting: Somalia's Difficult Decade, 1980–1990, Harrying the Hawiye."
12. Makinda, *Seeking Peace from Chaos*, 25–27.
13. "Somalia beyond the Warlords."
14. Press Release, Somali Community of the Americas.
15. "Somalia beyond the Warlords."
16. Makinda, *Seeking Peace from Chaos*, 43.
17. Ibid., 42.
18. "Somalia beyond the Warlords."
19. Salih and Wohlgemuth, *Crisis Management*, 12–16.
20. Clarke, "Failed Visions," 4–6.
21. Cassanelli, "Somali Land Resource Issues," 67–69.
22. Clarke, "Failed Visions," 6.
23. Sahnoun, *Somalia*, 5.
24. Clarke, "Failed Visions," 7.
25. Sahnoun, *Somalia*, 5–6.
26. Ibid., 81.
27. Ibid., 8.
28. Ibid., 7–8.
29. "Somalia beyond the Warlords."
30. Sahnoun, *Somalia*, 8.
31. Ibid., 9–10.
32. Rotberg, "The Lessons of Somalia," 235.
33. Woods, "U.S. Government Decisionmaking Processes," 151–53.
34. UN Office for the Coordination of Humanitarian Affairs, "IRIN [Integrated Regional Information Networks] Webspecial."
35. Clarke, "Failed Visions," 6.
36. Drysdale, "Foreign Military Intervention," 118–21.
37. Ibid., 122–24.
38. Brune, *The United States and Post–Cold War Interventions*, 17–18.
39. Ibid.
40. Sahnoun, *Somalia*, 39.
41. Hippel, *Democracy by Force*, 62.
42. Brune, *The United States and Post–Cold War Interventions*, 18–19.
43. Drysdale, "Foreign Military Intervention," 126–27.
44. Hippel, *Democracy by Force*, 169.
45. Menkhaus and Ortmayer, *Key Decisions*, 2.
46. Woods, "U.S. Government Decisionmaking Processes," 155.

47. Menkhaus and Ortmayer, *Key Decisions*, 3–4.
48. Woods, "U.S. Government Decisionmaking Processes," 155–56.
49. "Military: Operation Provide Relief," *GlobalSecurity.org*.
50. Hutcheson, *Air Mobility*, 90.
51. Menkhaus and Ortmayer, *Key Decisions*, 4.
52. Hutcheson, *Air Mobility*, 90.
53. Menkhaus and Ortmayer, *Key Decisions*, 4.
54. Hutcheson, *Air Mobility*, 90.
55. Woods, "U.S. Government Decisionmaking Processes," 156–57.
56. Menkhaus and Ortmayer, *Key Decisions*, 6.
57. Sommer, *Hope Restored?* 30.
58. Menkhaus and Ortmayer, *Key Decisions*, 6–7.
59. Ibid., 8.
60. Makinda, *Seeking Peace from Chaos*, 70–71.
61. Menkhaus and Ortmayer, *Key Decisions*, 11–12.
62. Clarke, "Failed Visions," 9.
63. Brune, *The United States and Post–Cold War Interventions*, 23–24.
64. Sommer, *Hope Restored?* 37–38.
65. Woods, "U.S. Government Decisionmaking Processes," 160.
66. Brune, *The United States and Post–Cold War Interventions*, 21–22.
67. Menkhaus and Ortmayer, *Key Decisions*, 12.
68. Drysdale, "Foreign Military Intervention,"127–28.
69. Woods, "U.S. Government Decisionmaking Processes," 159.
70. Makinda, *Seeking Peace from Chaos*, 74–75.
71. Sommer, *Hope Restored?* 39.
72. Drysdale, "Foreign Military Intervention,"131.
73. Ibid., 132.
74. Woods, "U.S. Government Decisionmaking Processes," 164–65.
75. Sommer, *Hope Restored?* 41.
76. Woods, "U.S. Government Decisionmaking Processes," 164.
77. Menkhaus and Ortmayer, *Key Decisions*, 16–17.
78. Woods, "U.S. Government Decisionmaking Processes," 163.
79. Ibid., 165.
80. Howe, "Relations between the United States and the UN in Somalia," 183.
81. Tomlinson, "US General Calls Somalia Terror Haven."
82. Clarke and Herbst, "Somalia and the Future of Humanitarian Intervention," 239.
83. Joint Publication (JP) 3-07.6, *Joint Tactics, Techniques, and Procedures for Foreign Humanitarian Assistance*, I-7–I-8.
84. US Department of Defense, *National Defense Strategy of the United States of America*, 3.
85. Ghormley, "Command Philosophy."
86. Weiss, "Rekindling Hope," 216–17.
87. A Theater Security Cooperation Plan is a strategic planning document intended to link a combatant commander's regional engagement activities with national strategic objectives. For more information, see JP 3-0, *Doctrine for Joint Operations: Revision Final Coordination*, I-7 and I-5–I-6.

88. Brune, *The United States and Post–Cold War Interventions*, 34.
89. Menkhaus and Ortmayer, *Key Decisions*, 12.
90. Clarke and Herbst, "Somalia and the Future of Humanitarian Intervention," 247.
91. Rotberg, "The Lessons of Somalia," 233.
92. Hirsch and Oakley, *Somalia and Operation Restore Hope*, 164.
93. Clarke and Herbst, "Somalia and the Future of Humanitarian Intervention," 250.
94. Woods, "U.S. Government Decisionmaking Processes," 169.
95. Howe, "Relations between the United States and the UN in Somalia," 186.
96. Crocker, "The Lessons of Somalia," 8.
97. Clarke and Herbst, "Somalia and the Future of Humanitarian Intervention," 242–43.
98. Woods, "U.S. Government Decisionmaking Processes," 169.
99. Hirsch and Oakley, *Somalia and Operation Restore Hope*, 166–67.
100. JP 3-07.6, *Joint Doctrine for Military Operations Other Than War*, I-8.
101. Clarke and Herbst, "Somalia and the Future of Humanitarian Intervention," 243.
102. Rotberg, "The Lessons of Somalia," 235.
103. Hirsch and Oakley, *Somalia and Operation Restore Hope*, 154.
104. Hippel, *Democracy by Force*, 83.
105. Allard, *Somalia Operations*, 90.
106. Clarke, "Failed Visions," 10–11.
107. Clarke and Herbst, "Somalia and the Future of Humanitarian Intervention," 246–47.
108. Betts, "Delusion of Impartial Intervention."
109. Allard, *Somalia Operations*, 9.
110. Clarke and Herbst, "Somalia and the Future of Humanitarian Intervention," 244–45.
111. Kennedy, "The Military and Humanitarian Organizations," 100.
112. Ibid., 114–15.
113. JP 3-57, *Joint Doctrine for Civil-Military Operations*, IV-2.
114. JP 3-07, *Joint Doctrine for Military Operations Other Than War*, II-3.
115. Hicks, "Fire in the City," 81–82.
116. Purvis, "One Lesson Worth Remembering," 45.
117. Hicks, "Fire in the City," 78–79.
118. Ibid., 80.
119. Carr, "The Consequences of Somalia," 3–4.
120. Denning, "Creating an Effective African Standby Force."
121. Berman and Sams, *Peacekeeping in Africa*, 260–63.
122. Henk and Metz, *United States and the Transformation of African Security*, 9.
123. Denning, "Creating an Effective African Standby Force."
124. Cilliers and Malan, "Progress with the African Standby Force."
125. Ibid.
126. Kent and Malan, "The African Standby Force: Progress and Prospects," 78.

127. de Coning, "Refining the African Standby Force Concept," 24.
128. "Cost and Steps for Establishing and Operationalising the African Standby Force," *Institute for Security Studies*.
129. "Fact Sheet: Iraqi War" *InfoPlease Almanacs*.
130. "Operations and Initiatives," *US European Command*.
131. Carafano and Gardiner, "U.S. Military Assistance for Africa."
132. Denning, "Creating an Effective African Standby Force."

Case Study 2

Genocide, Airpower, and Intervention

Rwanda 1994

Maj George Stanley, USAF

In response to a question about believing in God, Lt Gen Roméo Dallaire, commander of the United Nations peacekeeping force in Rwanda, known as the UN Assistance Mission in Rwanda (UNAMIR), stated that he had shaken hands with the devil in Rwanda, and since he knew the devil existed, he had to believe in God.[1] While most Americans simply changed the channel during news broadcasts of the savage violence that decimated Rwanda, the 2,548 members of UNAMIR and the estimated 800,000 people that were murdered during 100 days of organized killing could not. In the aftermath of this tragedy, four questions emerged.

- Why was genocide pursued as a final solution?
- How did the relatively small group most committed to implementing genocide gain cooperation from the populace at large?
- Why did the United States and United Nations not intervene?
- Could the United States have intervened effectively?

These questions frame the following analysis of the Rwandan genocide of 1994. Most of the debate about Rwanda has focused on the lack of political will to stop the genocide. Only a handful of studies analyze the military capability of the international community to intervene in Rwanda effectively. Specifically, how might US airpower have played critical roles in transporting intervention forces, providing strike and reconnaissance capabilities, and shutting down perpetrator communications and radio?

Why Genocide?

In order to understand genocide in Rwanda, one should examine Rwanda's colonial history and how the ethnic conflict between the Hutus and Tutsis developed. The first European explorers contacted Rwandan society in the late nineteenth century and found a homogeneous society divided into three main groups: Hutu, Tutsi, and Twa. These groups shared the same Bantu language, intermarried, and fought side-by-side to defend or extend the Rwanda kingdom. Rwanda had its share of wars and violence, but "there is no trace in [Rwanda's] precolonial history of systematic violence between Tutsi and Hutu as such."[2]

However, each group acquired a separate stereotype in appearance and social status. The Twa were approximately 1 percent of the population, and were pygmoid hunter-gatherers whose only social opportunity was in serving the king of Rwanda or other patrons.[3] The Hutu comprised approximately 85 percent of the population, and were peasant farmers with the standard Bantu physical features attributed to residents of central and southern Africa.[4] Early European explorers described the Hutu as short, stocky, and round-faced with flat noses and thick lips.[5] By contrast, the Tutsi were described as typically extremely tall and thin with angular facial features more akin to the Europeans. They were associated with herding cattle.[6] Fixation on these differences would become the basis for ethnic conflict between the Hutus and the Tutsis.

In reality it is very difficult to distinguish between a Hutu and a Tutsi based on physical attributes. Some studies argue that the word Tutsi at first referred to the ruling elite, while the word Hutu at first referred to contempt for inferiors, regardless of race.[7] The difference was really more of a social separation—farmers and cattle herders. In early Rwandan society, a Hutu could actually become somewhat "Tutsified" by receiving cattle as a gift from his patron while a Tutsi who lost all of his cattle and had to farm the land could become "Hutuised."[8] While this was not a common occurrence since much depended on the generosity of the Tutsi patron and Hutu were not supposed to own cattle, movement in either direction could occur by marriage. A successful Hutu might marry into a Tutsi lineage or a struggling Tutsi marry into a Hutu lineage.[9] The distinction between Hutu and Tutsi was made more sharp and hostile with the colonial influence of Europe.

Both the German and Belgian colonizers focused almost exclusively on the physical differences between the Hutu and Tutsi, assuming that the Tutsi were superior and naturally inclined to lead in the same way that Europeans were presumed to be superior to Africans.[10] This led to the conclusions that the Tutsis were natural-born leaders with gifted intelligence when compared to the Hutus.[11] Some went so far as to claim the Tutsis had Semitic origins, were descendants from the Garden of Eden, the lost continent of Atlantis, or even visitors from outer space.[12] These European theories and assumptions eventually led the Tutsi to believe they really were a superior race and the Hutu to develop a severe inferiority complex.[13] This condition was made significantly worse by changes in the way Rwanda was governed.

Traditional Rwandan government consisted of a king with numerous chiefs that fell into three different categories: chiefs of the landholdings, chiefs of men, or chiefs of the pastures. While most of these chiefs were Tutsi, many of the chiefs of the landholdings were Hutu since that area included agricultural production, and other chief positions were usually assigned to different men in an attempt to complicate the balance of power and provide checks and balances while subduing a difficult area or hill. Additionally, this afforded the Hutus with some ability to influence local politics even if most of the chiefs were Tutsi.[14]

German and Belgian colonialists found it difficult to exert their control within this complex system and worked to drastically change the administration, to improve efficiency, and to shift completely the balance of power.[15] The German and Belgian influences on Rwandan society were very different. Germany ruled Rwanda indirectly from 1897 to 1916, leaving a large degree of leeway to the leadership of the Rwandan monarchy.[16] While they did not make deep changes in Rwandan society, the Germans began the process of shifting power towards the Tutsi chiefs.[17] Ten years after taking control in 1916 and attempting futilely to put Hutus into chiefly positions, Belgian authorities began a series of reform measures that eventually fused all three chiefly offices into one and replaced almost all Hutu chiefs with Tutsi chiefs.[18] Rwandan society, once characterized by overlapping and intersecting spheres of authority based on family compounds associated with a high ground or hill (Rwandans describe their country as the "land of the 1,000 hills"), became increasingly defined in terms of Hutu and Tutsi identity. By systematically dismantling the traditional and complex "hill" hierarchy structure, the Belgians gave Tutsi leaders absolute power over Hutu vassals.[19] Belgian authorities also instituted ethnic identification cards that specified whether a citizen was a Hutu, Tutsi, or Twa.[20] In this way, Hutu peasants found themselves at the mercy of one chief, usually a Tutsi, backed by a brutal white administration.

The process of extracting taxes and forced labor from citizens for public works changed drastically as well. Under traditional Rwandan rule, when a royal chief required labor from a certain hill, the hill would choose a worker or workers to fulfill the obligation.[21] The Belgians extended that obligation, requiring that every man, and sometimes women and children, work. By 1940 the burden had increased to the point where men were so exhausted from constant communal labor that they were unable to tend to their own fields, resulting in numerous episodes of famine.[22] Anyone who did not cooperate was brutally beaten. A UN Trusteeship Mandate Delegation to Rwanda interrogated 250 peasants in 1948 and found that 247 of them had been beaten, usually more than once.[23] Colonial authorities felt no compunction about publicly whipping local Tutsi chiefs when work quotas were missed, with the chiefs then taking out their anger on their Hutu subordinates.[24] One elderly Tutsi remembered a Belgian colonial order to, "whip the Hutu or we will whip you."[25]

Some higher-level Tutsi, knowing they had the backing of the Belgian government, began to change the traditional land and contractual relationships between patron and peasant.[26] Belgian lawmakers introduced legislation that designated undivided usufruct land not actually occupied by the natives (the Hutu) as legally vacant, allowing the state and the Tutsi chiefs to gain control of traditional Hutu landholdings after very miserly "due compensation."[27] Although this abuse was limited to high-lineage Tutsi who were in position to work with and benefit from the Belgian legislation, most Hutu peasants came to view all Tutsi as greedy oppressors.

Education was another area of conflict between the Hutu and the Tutsi. The Roman Catholic Church generally provided a quality education, but it was limited to those who could afford it and typically was reserved to Tutsi students, since they were assumed to be racially superior and naturally destined to lead their Hutu counterparts.[28] This resulted in high illiteracy rates and frustration among the few Hutus that managed to become students, since they could not get jobs equivalent to their level of education.[29] Although the Belgians possessed overall authority over Rwanda, a small group of Tutsi gained a monopoly on local administration, which they used to further their own interests.[30]

All of these actions were legitimized by the supposed racial superiority of the Tutsi. High-lineage Tutsi took advantage of their Belgian sponsorship to further their own interests, and even marginally influential Tutsi accepted the myth that they were inherently superior to the Hutu.[31] The Hutu were left "deprived of all political power and materially exploited by both the whites and the Tutsi, told by everyone that they were inferiors who deserved their fate." They began to believe it, beginning to hate all Tutsi regardless of political or economic status, simply because they were Tutsi. "The time-bomb had been set and it was now only a question of when it would go off."[32]

In the 1950s the relationships between the Tutsi, the Belgians, the church, and the Hutu began to shift slightly. Under UN pressure to end colonial rule, Belgian administrators began to incorporate Hutus into responsible positions and admit more Hutu into secondary schools.[33] The Tutsi elite began to imagine the end of colonial rule and independence and realized that their position in society could be jeopardized if they waited too long for Belgium to transfer power.[34]

The first liberalizing measures envisioned free elections for councils at every administrative level. In practice chiefs and subchiefs (generally Tutsis) nominated the candidates and thereby controlled the electoral process.[35] These measures moved power from the Belgians to the elite Tutsis, and while these elite Tutsi were beginning to challenge Belgian authority, a Hutu middle class was emerging.

The leadership of the Church supported Tutsi dominance until the late 1930s. After World War II, Belgian clergymen of lower middle and working class origins began to sympathize with the Hutu majority.[36] Additionally, a growing Hutu counter-elite received economic opportunity and leadership training from the 1956 creation of the TRAFIPRO (*Travail, fidélité, progrès'* or work, fidelity, progress) coffee cooperative and began to organize and create security societies and cultural associations.[37] In March 1957, Hutu intellectuals published the "Bahutu Manifesto" which embraced the myth of the Tutsi as foreign invaders and argued that Rwanda was a nation of the Hutu majority.[38] Moreover, the manifesto supported identity cards that specified Tutsi, Hutu, or Twa ethnicity to clearly demonstrate that the Hutu were the majority in Rwanda.[39] The Tutsi elite responded in a highly emotional defensive reaction and political rivalry and maneuvering quickly went beyond reason.[40]

Among the political parties that sprouted in the late 1950s were the Hutu Social Movement (*Mouvement Social Muhutu* or MSM), known later as the Democratic Republican Movement–Party of the Movement for the Emancipation of the Hutu People (*Mouvement Démocratique Républicain–Parti du Mouvement de l'Emancipation du Peuple Hutu* or MDR-PARMEHUTU), and the Association for the Social Promotion of the Masses (*Association Pour la Promotion Sociale de la Masse* or APROSOMA) founded by Hutus. The Rwandese National Union (*Union Nationale Rwandaise* UNAR) consisting of Tutsi conservatives, was openly anti-Belgian, and supported immediate Rwandan independence. Cold War reasoning prompted communist members of the UN Trusteeship Council to support UNAR since they were against the Belgians and therefore the West in general. Hostility between the Tutsi elite and Belgian authorities deepened.[41] Unfortunately the ensuing political maneuvering was never really about reconciling the ethnically bipolar state, and it was only a matter of time before violence erupted.[42]

In November 1959 a MDR-PARMEHUTU activist was severely beaten by young UNAR members, immediately prompting Hutu activists to attack Tutsi chiefs and UNAR members.[43] Tutsi houses were burned regardless of whether or not they were elite Tutsi. UNAR members retaliated against Hutu activists.[44]

The violence, known as "the wind of destruction," lasted for two weeks. Belgian authorities showed extreme favoritism toward the Hutu activists, standing by while they burned Tutsi homes.[45] Before the elections in mid-1960, the violence continued, with the Tutsis receiving the worst of it. Belgian authorities began replacing Tutsi chiefs with Hutus, who immediately sought revenge on their Tutsi oppressors.[46]

Communal elections took place in mid-1960, with Hutus presiding over the polling stations, resulting in Hutu parties, especially MDR-PARMEHUTU and APROSOMA, winning over 90 percent of the new government seats compared to less than 2 percent for UNAR.[47] The new burgomasters controlled 229 communes, of which 160 were MDR-PARMEHUTU, and only 19 were Tutsi. In the face of criticism from the United Nations and from the communist countries supporting UNAR, Belgian authorities arranged a declaration of independence for the Republic of Rwanda while anti-Tutsi violence continued. In the legislative elections of 1961 the MDR-PARMEHUTU won 78 percent of the vote and 35 of 44 seats in the government.[48] According to a UN report, "The developments of these last eighteen months have brought about the racial dictatorship of one party. . . . An oppressive system has been replaced by another one. . . . It is quite possible that some day we will witness violent reactions on the part of the Tutsi."[49]

Rwanda's democratic revolution emphasized "the intrinsic worth of being Hutu, the total congruence between demographic majority and democracy, the need to follow a moral Christian life, and the uselessness of politics which should be replaced by hard work."[50] This was essentially the ideology of the former Belgian/Tutsi rule of Rwanda turned on its head. Following Rwanda's independence, Hutu leaders put the concept of an ethnically based quota system, enunciated in the 1957 Bahutu Manifesto, into practice. Tutsis, officially constituting 9 percent of the population of Rwanda, would henceforth be limited to 9 percent of the jobs in any one sector and only 9 percent of school enrollment.[51]

Anti-Tutsi violence in Rwanda continued sporadically from 1959 until the genocide in 1994; and as a result, an estimated 600,000 to 700,000 Tutsis fled from Rwanda to Burundi, Uganda, Tanzania, and the Democratic Republic of Congo (formerly known as Zaire).[52] As early as late 1960, small bands of exiled Tutsis began commando raids from Uganda, each time causing violent reprisals against Tutsi civilians still living in Rwanda.[53] These groups were referred to as *inyenzi*, or cockroaches, by the Hutu, a reference that played a part in 1994.[54] Success of the exiles depended largely on where they lived, with the most successful being in Burundi, where the new leaders sympathized with the Tutsi while Uganda and Tanzania tightly controlled the Tutsi, to prevent their military operations.[55] The exiles were able to launch an offensive from Burundi in late 1963 that nearly reached Kigali, the capital of Rwanda but was quickly beaten back and resulted in the deaths of around 10,000 Tutsi, including all the Tutsi politicians still living in Rwanda.[56] Hutu extremists would refer to the Tutsi refugees that escaped Rwanda as "the mistake of 1960," since those refugees grew into the Rwandan Patriotic Front (RPF), which will be described later.[57]

Exile politics in Rwanda died in 1964 and remained dead until 1979 when Tutsi refugees in Uganda formed the Rwandese Refugee Welfare Foundation, which evolved into the more militant Rwandese Alliance for National Unity (RANU).[58] RANU was forced out of Uganda from 1981 until 1986 due to civil war within Uganda, but during that time many Tutsi soldiers fought with the National Resistance Army against the government of Uganda, gaining crucial combat and leadership experience.[59] In fact, the rebel leader, Yoweri Museveni, had several thousand Rwandan Tutsis in his army in January 1986 when he defeated the brutal dictator Milton Obote and was sworn in as president of Uganda.[60] After returning to Uganda in 1987, the RANU was renamed the RPF responding to increased repression of Rwandan refugees, mostly Tutsi, in Uganda. The RPF committed itself to returning the exiles to Rwanda.[61]

In October 1990, 2,500 RPF troops wearing Ugandan army uniforms invaded Rwanda.[62] The attack stalled after only two days of fighting, and the Rwandan government forces, with help from French, Belgian, and Zairian forces, forced the entire RPF force to desert or retreat into Uganda by the end of October.[63] While the operation nearly destroyed the RPF, it did strike fear into the Hutu elite of Rwanda and caused a massive recruitment of soldiers.[64] While weapons were not a problem since France provided them, discipline in the government forces eventually weakened by mid-1992. In the meantime, RPF forces rested, regrouped, and gained volunteers from all over the world, eventually growing to almost 12,000 troops by the end of 1992 and still growing.[65]

When the RPF attacked again from Uganda in February 1992, the undisciplined Rwandan government forces were forced to retreat, and the advance stopped 30 kilometers north of Kigali only when RPF leaders declared a unilateral cease-fire due to France's declared support of Pres. Juvénal Habyarimana and his government in Kigali. Government forces were clearly unable to defend the capital against the RPF without French support. While thousands of Hutu peasants fled from the Tutsi army, extremist and moderate Hutu politicians alike feared a return to the Tutsi oppression of 40 years earlier. While differences between Hutu and Tutsi were artificial, they were very real and tangible by the early 1990s and would be translated into fear, hatred, and action.[66]

The second ingredient is the devaluation of human life, which coincides with the course of ethnic conflict between the Tutsis and Hutus since 1960. There had been a population explosion within Rwanda together with the constant cycle of attacks and reprisals between the two groups. The population of Rwanda increased from almost 1.6 million in 1934 to over 7.1 million in 1989.[67] This resulted in an increase from approximately 61 people per square kilometer to 270 people per square kilometer, making Rwanda the most densely populated nation on the African continent.[68] Although the decision to pursue genocide was primarily political, the already intense competition for land and resources increased exponentially when coffee and tin prices crashed in the mid-1980s.[69]

As previously noted, anti-Tutsi violence began with the political maneuverings of the late 1950s and continued in response to RPF attacks. Hutu peasants participated in all of the small-scale massacres of Tutsi civilians from 1990 through 1994. However, there are several examples of anti-Hutu violence at the hands of Tutsis in the region as well. In 1972 the Tutsi ruling elite in Rwanda's southern neighbor, Burundi, set out to kill every Hutu male over 14 years of age along with every Hutu cabinet member and government officer, resulting in the massacre of an estimated 200,000 Hutus.[70] Hutu massacres in Burundi at the hands of Tutsi killers were repeated in 1988 and 1991, while RPF advances also included reprisals against suspected Hutu extremists.[71] Additionally, under the Habyarimana regime, dissent and subversion were severely punished, and the few people who tried to expose government corruption during the economic crisis were killed, many by car accidents with strange circumstances.[72] Murder and rape became common occurrences in Rwanda and neighboring countries as respect for human life decreased and hatred and mistrust intensified.

One of the last, and arguably one of most important, ingredients for genocide in Rwanda, was the rise of the intransigent Hutu power party named the *Coalition Pour la Defense de la République* (CDR). Members of the CDR allied with a powerful inner circle known as the *Akazu* ("small house," originally a reference to the inner circle of the king's court), consisting of the family and associates of President Habyarimana's wife.[73] The CDR and the *Akazu* worked publicly and behind the scenes to aggravate Hutu fear and distrust of the Tutsis, warning that an RPF victory would result in the resurrection of the pre-independence Tutsi overlordship. When the RPF first attacked in 1990, the Hutu elite panicked and initiated massacres of Tutsis inside Rwanda as *ibyitso* (accomplices).[74] The Tutsi threat appeared to manifest itself outside Rwanda as well, when Melchior Ndadaye, a Hutu engineer elected as president of Tutsi-dominated Burundi in a free and fair election, was kidnapped and murdered in October 1993, after only four months in office, by extremist Tutsi military officers.[75] The ensuing violence in Burundi killed approximately 50,000 people, Hutu and Tutsi, and caused some 300,000 Hutu refugees to flee to Rwanda with stories of massacre committed by the Tutsi army of Burundi.[76]

The CDR and influential members of the *Akazu* became increasingly alarmed that a negotiated settlement between the government of Rwanda and the RPF would open the road for renewed Tutsi domination of Rwanda and imperil their position within Rwanda. They viewed the Arusha Accords, signed in October 1993, with fear and distrust. At Arusha, representatives of the RPF and Habyarimana's government had agreed to a framework for ending the fighting between the RPF and the

Forces of the Rwandese Army (*Forces Armées Rwandaises* or FAR), forming a provisional government, repatriating refugees, and holding free elections. Hutu radicals feared that Habyarimana's stalling tactics could not long endure and believed that the president was about to succumb to international pressure to implement Arusha. They envisioned an alternate approach: the best way to deal with the Tutsi threat of the RPF, the problems of refugees, and international pressure, was to eliminate the Tutsis completely.[77] Hutu extremists believed they could get away with genocide as long as they could generate general popular support for the genocide, maintain efficiency during the killing, prevent the United Nations from intervening, and resist the RPF militarily.[78] On 6 April 1994, President Habyarimana's plane was shot down as it approached the Kigali airport carrying both Habyarimana and the president of Burundi. Habyarimana was returning from a meeting in Dar es Salaam, where regional leaders had pressed him to move forward with implementing the Arusha Accords. Roadblocks immediately began to spring up in Kigali as Hutu opponents of the Arusha Accords began to implement their plan of committing genocide on a massive scale. Over the course of the next 100 days, some 800,000 Tutsis would be methodically killed alongside thousands of Hutu moderates.[79]

Popular Cooperation

To understand the role of the general populace in the Rwandan genocide, the role of propaganda and its effectiveness in gaining cooperation, compliance, or at least noninterference of the populace needs to be explored. Shortly after the Arusha peace accords were signed, the Hutu extremist radio station, Thousand Hills Independent Radio and Television (*Radio Télévision Libre Mille Collines* or RTLMC), began broadcasting its hate propaganda that would lead to genocide.[80] Other propaganda sources were available, like the paper *Kangura* (*Wake Them Up*), but more than 60 percent of Rwanda's population was illiterate. The radio, which was easily the most powerful medium, could be received throughout most of Rwanda.[81] In addition to preaching racism through street slang, obscene jokes, and good music, RTLMC openly criticized President

Habyarimana for being too soft in dealing with the RPF rebels while inciting memories of halcyon majority democracy and evil Tutsi feudalist enslavement.[82] RTLMC reported the assassination of Burundi president Ndadaye with urgent calls for action. By April 1994, RTLMC had managed to convince Hutus that killing was communal work, with killing men equivalent to bush clearing and killing women and children equivalent to pulling out the roots of bad weeds.[83] Later, reporting the shoot down of President Habyarimana's aircraft as committed by RPF terrorists, the radio station urged murderous vengeance and took on a life of its own, becoming the voice of genocide.[84]

Cooperation included not only actual killing, but also manning roadblocks and informing on Tutsi hideouts. Many Hutu cooperated out of greed or because they believed the Tutsi threat to be real. Others cooperated because of Rwandan's tradition of strict obedience to the government. Still others cooperated for fear of their own safety or in order to save their Tutsi wives.[85] Whatever the reason, an estimated 50,000 Hutus, organized into militia groups such as the *Interahamwe* (those who stand together), participated in the slaughter. Stories told by the killers include tales of killing women, children, and neighbors with guns, grenades, and machetes, and yet the focus is on the fact that meat and food were readily available and killing was actually more productive than farming.[86] It is important to note, also, that the estimated 800,000 dead does not include the victims who did not die from their wounds and the number of women and girls raped.[87] However, there were some instances of resistance.

The most well-known example is that of Paul and Tatiana Rusesabagina, portrayed in the movie *Hotel Rwanda*. Through bribery with money and alcohol, Paul was able to save his family and nearly 1,000 Tutsis hiding out in the *Hôtel Mille des Collines*.[88] A number of priests and Christian workers resisted militia efforts to round up Tutsi hiding in churches or schools, and in some cases they were killed along with their charges.[89] In another instance, an *Interahamwe* leader actually saved almost everyone on his hill by telling authorities he had already killed all of the enemies.[90] There were several accounts of Hutu individuals helping Tutsi survivors by hiding them or supplying food, but this was publicly prohibited, and those who were caught received the same brutal treatment as the fugitives they fostered.[91] These examples were, unfortunately, the exception, not the rule.

Efficiency, maintained by premeditated planning and practice, was important in order to eliminate the Tutsi before the RPF could advance to stop the operation or the outside world could see the tragedy through the fog of civil war and intervene. The premeditation of the killings is evidenced by the appearance of *Interahamwe* roadblocks in Kigali less than an hour after President Habyarimana's plane was shot down, the strident broadcasts that same evening on RTLMC to avenge the president's death and fill the graves completely, as well as the death lists the presidential guard carried during their first days of killing.[92] These lists ensured that leaders like Prime Minister Agathe Uwilingiyimana, president of the Constitutional Court Joseph Kavaruganda, and all opposition party members were killed first.[93] With the opposition eliminated, the genocide planners installed a provisional government consisting entirely of Hutu power extremists, which appointed an army officer to each prefecture to direct local killings in the name of civil defense.[94] According to one of the killers named Pancrace, "Rule number one was to kill. There was no rule number two. It was an organization without complications."[95]

April 1994 was not the first time that groups of Hutus had organized and massacred Tutsis. There were at least nine rehearsal slaughters, beginning as early as October 1990 through January 1993, which killed an estimated 2,000 Tutsis and accomplice Hutus in more than 12 different communes.[96] These practices not only helped the groups gain leadership and execution experience, but also reinforced the tradition of unquestioning obedience to authority in Rwanda.[97] The degree of efficiency achieved is clear from the massacres in the Kibuye Province in the west, which saw over 200,000 of its estimated 250,000 Tutsis killed.[98]

US/UN Nonintervention

The United Nations originally planned to enter Rwanda under the UN Observer Mission Uganda-Rwanda (UNAMUR), but the mission changed to UN Assistance Mission for Rwanda as a peacekeeping force shortly after the Arusha Accords were signed.[99] Debates over the appropriate size of the force ranged from 500 to 8,000 soldiers, and only Belgium seemed willing to commit the preponderance of troops.[100] UNAMIR's budget was not formally approved until 4 April 1994, just two days before the genocide began, leaving UNAMIR pitifully short on medicine, food, ammunition, and armored personnel carriers.[101] As the genocide unfolded, Lieutenant General Dallaire stated that the rules of engagement allowed the use of deadly force to prevent crimes against humanity, but the responses he received from UN headquarters forbade using force unless fired upon and stressed negotiation to avoid conflict above all else.[102] The reasons for the timidity in allocating troops, equipment, or money, lay in another African country to the northeast.

United Nations Security Council Resolution 794 was signed in December 1992, creating the mandate that led to Operation Restore Hope and an attempt to deliver relief supplies to the southern areas of Somalia. While this mission included US marines as part of the UNITAF, it was made very clear that deploying the marines was strictly a humanitarian event, and as such they would only use force in defense of themselves and food convoys. As tensions grew between the warlord Aideed and Ambassador Oakley, the Security Council passed a resolution that transitioned Restore Hope to UNOSOM II which widened the scope from purely humanitarian to forceful intervention in order to secure all of Somalia. After instances of bloodshed against Pakistani peacekeepers, the intervention shifted from a neutral humanitarian force to a war against Aideed. The climax occurred in the US Rangers' and Special Forces commandos' attempt to capture Aideed, which resulted in the deaths of 18 Americans and about 200 Somalis along with the shootdown and capture of three American Blackhawk helicopters broadcast on CNN.[103]

Presidential Decision Directed 25 was a result of the Somalia experience, significantly reforming US policy on getting involved in peace operations. While it was not signed until May 1994, it was in draft process and on the minds of policy makers as the Rwandan genocide unfolded.[104] When the 10 Belgian UNAMIR soldiers who were guarding Prime Minister Uwilingiyimana were murdered, it only seemed to reinforce the lessons learned from

Somalia.[105] Although the United States was ready to withdraw UNAMIR completely on 7 April 1994, it was the departure of the Belgians, the former colonial ruler, and resident experts on Rwanda, that signaled that the West had little appetite for intervention.

Additionally, Rwanda was not the only crisis du jour. President Clinton's administration was busy handling unrest in Bosnia, Iraq, and, much closer to home with more probability for success, in Haiti.[106] The simple fact was there seemed to be no vital American interests in Africa after the end of the Cold War, and Western media did not provide graphic images until it was too late. This was due to efforts of the Hutu killers to mask the genocide until after the evacuation of most Western journalists on 14 April 1994. Press reports about the killings generally described them as tribal or ethnic violence within the context of a vicious civil war, supporting arguments that only an overwhelmingly large intervention force could have stopped the killing, an option that seemed to be out of the question. Even in May 1994, after the genocide had been publicly revealed and Lieutenant General Dallaire had requested 5,500 reinforcements for UNAMIR's dwindling forces, the will to intervene remained low. Just prior to the vote on the matter, a representative from Rwanda spoke to the General Assembly, describing the killings as an interethnic war caused by years of ruthless Tutsi domination of the Hutu majority.[107] The Security Council voted to authorize the increase in UNAMIR troops, but that is all it was, an authorization—no troops were ever deployed due to arguments over who would pay for the operation and whether or not it would remain a peacekeeping operation or transition to peace enforcement.[108]

Intervention and Airpower

The first step to determining whether or not the United States could have intervened involves determining when our leadership could have realistically known that Rwanda was in the throes of genocide and reacted appropriately. One argument is that, based on extensive open-source reporting during the first two weeks of the genocide, ". . . the president of the United States could not have determined that a nationwide genocide was under way in Rwanda until about April 20th."[109] However, this assumes complete ignorance of any ethnic hostility or plans of genocide within Rwanda. Lieutenant General Dallaire had actually been contacted by a leader of the *Interahamwe*, code-named Jean-Pierre, who spoke of lists of Tutsi victims as well as a plan to exterminate the Tutsi in Rwanda and offered to reveal the four arms caches in Kigali to UNAMIR troops.[110] The informant even mentioned a plan to kill some Belgian soldiers in order to force them to withdraw from Rwanda and effectively prevent the West and the United Nations from intervening.[111] Although Dallaire's request to raid these caches was denied, the request should have signaled the prospect of genocide to New York and Washington. Three months later, when widespread violence broke out and 10 Belgian peacekeepers were killed, it should have been seen as a confirmation of Jean-Pierre's report to Dallaire.

In defense of the decision makers, this was a definite case of information overload and very real confusion over whether or not the massacres were genocide or a natural result of renewed civil war, but it is possible that policy makers in Belgium, the United States, France, and the United Nations understood or at least suspected the threat of genocide.[112] Before evacuating the country, journalists described the violence as systematic killings on an ethnic basis, and as early as 8 April, Lieutenant General Dallaire sent a cable to the United Nations requesting permission to transition to a chapter 7 operation.[113] Based on a discussion paper on Rwanda, dated 1 May, that specifically warned against "signing up to troop contributions" and being careful about actually using the word *genocide* because it could force the United States to "do something," it is very likely that policy makers knew a mass killing or genocide was occurring in Rwanda but lacked the political will to intervene.[114] As a result nothing happened, and genocide proceeded as planned. One official remarked, "Everyone knew, even in Belgium, what was going to happen because the organization of the genocide had been in place for a long time."[115]

Assuming that the international community knew that Rwandan Tutsis were the objects of systematic genocide by 20 April 1994, could the increase in UNAMIR troops really have made a difference? Col Scott Feil, summarizing the conclusions of a 1997 Carnegie Commission conference tasked with considering whether "the introduction of international military force into the situation in Rwanda in 1994 could have had any effect on the situation there," concluded that "based on the presentations by the panel and other research, the author believes that a modern force of 5,000 troops, drawn primarily from a single contributing country, and inserted between April 7th and 21st, could have significantly altered the outcome."[116] The panel assessed both General Dallaire's April 1994 proposal to "obtain reinforcements, stop the genocide, and bring the parties back to the [Arusha] peace process," and a more aggressive scheme that envisioned (1) interposing forces between the RPF and FAR, and (2) securing the capital and countryside through use of tactical and strategic air mobility.[117]

The conference's conclusion rested on the assumption that a "window of opportunity for the employment of such a force" existed from about 7 to 21 April 1994 and that "US participation would have been essential."[118] It is important to note that airlift would have been hard pressed to deliver combat capability within this time table. Sending a force of 5,000 troops closely corresponded to Dr. Alan J. Kuperman's "moderate intervention force" of 6,000 troops, which would have required 21 days to arrive.[119] Given the best-case notification of 8 April and following Dr. Kuperman's reasoning, those forces would not have arrived until 29 April after an estimated 250,000 Rwandans had already been killed.[120] While this moderate force could have saved 100,000 Tutsis, completely stopping the genocide would have required approximately 15,000 troops and an estimated 40 days of airlift.[121] While it would have been difficult to impossible to meet the 7 to 21 April window, any intervention would have likely saved thousands of Tutsi lives. Would the risks have been low?

The French intervention of late June through August 1994, Operation Turquoise, may not be the best yardstick to measure risk. The French intervention force was robust, numbering 2,500 soldiers, over 100 armored vehicles, artillery, helicopters, as well as ground-attack and reconnaissance aircraft.[122] However, the French forces encountered little resistance from the Rwandan government and its genocidal killers because many Hutus viewed the intervention as a repeat of 1990, when France intervened along with troops from Zaire to repel an RPF advance that threatened to reach Kigali.[123] As for the RPF, the French encountered no opposition from RPF troops because French units entered from Cyangugu, far to the southwest in Rwanda, well away from the RPF-FAR front lines. RPF envoys in Paris had been assured that heavy firepower would remain in Zaire unless French troops were attacked, and French units refused to be drawn into the civil war.[124] An earlier insertion of French forces directly into Kigali to stop the mass killings would have been much riskier, requiring a larger intervention force.

Airpower would have been vital to the success of any intervening force and could have mitigated the risk substantially in some areas while exposing new risks in other areas. Some of the capabilities airpower would have brought to the fight include airlift, electronic attack, direct attack/show of force, and reconnaissance. Airlift would be crucial for quickly delivering intervening troops and equipment, maintaining supply lines, and delivering humanitarian assistance for refugees and displaced persons. Airlift also could have mitigated the risk to personnel injured in combat operations, providing medical evacuation that might have saved the life of peacekeepers such as Uruguayan major Juan Saúl Sosa, who died an hour after a rocket attack on his vehicle, when the ambulance and armored personnel carrier sent to rescue him broke down.[125] With electronic attack, EC-130 Commando Solo aircraft could have removed the hate and murder messages of RTLMC from the airwaves and possibly replaced them with broadcasts to end the violence and portray the intervening force as truly neutral. This option was considered in early May 1994 but dismissed due to concerns over ineffectiveness versus cost and vulnerability of an aircraft with limited self-protection.[126]

Both airlift and electronic attack capabilities raise concerns for finding suitable airfield facilities and offload capabilities as well as force protection. Strategic airlift aircraft can carry more cargo than ever before, but they still require somewhat specialized equipment to offload palettes, store fuel, and process and protect warehouse supplies and equipment delivered. The only airport in Rwanda with that capability was Kigali International, right in the middle of the civil war and known to have had surface-to-air missiles fired at approaching aircraft. Other suitable airports include Bujumbura in Burundi and Entebbe and Gulu in Uganda. Although controlled by Tutsis, Burundi would have been exceptionally risky, considering the assassination of President Ndadaye some six months earlier. One of the airfields in Uganda would have been a better option for force protection, but the RPF had recently assisted the coup there, and working with the Ugandan government would have been viewed as collaboration with the Tutsis and resulted in the loss of perceived neutrality. Based on these observations, any deployment of aircraft would have required diplomatic support and dedicated security, but Entebbe in Uganda and Bujumbura in Burundi would have been the best staging areas. Only after friendly forces had secured the airport in Kigali could planners have begun using the Rwandan capital for operations.

The ability to provide show of force and direct attack would have provided immense firepower for light infantry or even mechanized forces. Show-of-force flights could have obviated ground combat and dispersed roadblocks and large groups of militia. This was true during Operation Provide Comfort in Iraq, when fighter aircraft would fly low over Iraqi units that were slow in withdrawing or orbit visibly during negotiations.[127] The psychological influence of aircraft overhead would have provided a strong deterrent and protective force for ground units or nongovernmental agencies conducting humanitarian assistance.[128] Interdiction could have been used in the form of punitive air strikes and might have coerced Rwanda's interim government leaders to stop the genocide and return to the Arusha Accords. This would have required detailed and accurate intelligence on what centers of gravity those leaders possessed.[129] However, an approach like the one taken in Operation Allied Force would not have been appropriate or effective for Rwanda, since Rwanda was not an industrialized nation like Serbia and there was still some question as to who was really in charge after President Habyarimana's assassination. The primary drawback of close air support and interdiction missions is the risk of collateral damage and injury to civilians within the most densely populated country in Africa.

A last consideration, but definitely not the least, is reconnaissance. Reconnaissance would have provided information on militia roadblocks and movements as well as RPF locations and concentrations. This knowledge would have been vital to massing the limited number of troops at decisive points or avoiding very large militant crowds. The MQ-1 Predator was used extensively in Operation Allied Force but, unfortunately, was still in development during the genocide of 1994.

Conclusion

Although the ethnic conflict between the Tutsi and the Hutu was not tribal but rather artificially created by the colonial influence of Germany and Belgium, the mistrust and hatred were very real by early 1994. Combined with a devaluation of human life, a small group of Hutu extremists used these factors to convince thousands of ordinary citizens that killing neighbors, family members, men, women, and children was no more than yard work. This does not and should not create an image of a primitive African society incapable of living in peace and prosperity, but rather an image of using genocide as a mean to a political end.

The United States and United Nations could have intervened and made a difference in the Rwanda genocide of 1994. However, the operation would have been medium to high risk and it is impossible to accurately estimate how many people could have been saved. Due to the lack of vital national interest in Central Africa and the recent experience in Somalia, with which every American with a television was familiar, convincing the American public of a need to intervene would have been difficult during the period when intervention would have been most effective.

Despite these reservations, the United States should have been the leading country in an intervention in Rwanda. The United States should have recognized that genocide was occurring, given the information that we possessed. We should have encouraged other nations, especially other African nations with a vested interest in stability in their region, to provide the troops and materiel for intervention and offered logistical, communications, and airpower support. We did nothing as hundreds of thousands were slaughtered. As Edmund Burke remarked two centuries ago, "All that is necessary for the triumph of evil is that good men do nothing."

Notes

1. Dallaire and Beardsley, *Shake Hands with the Devil*, xviii.
2. Prunier, *The Rwanda Crisis*, 5, 39.
3. Des Forges, *Leave None to Tell the Story*, 33–34.
4. Prunier, *Rwanda Crisis*, 5.
5. Gourevitch, *We Wish to Inform You*, 50.
6. Des Forges, *Leave None to Tell the Story*, 32–33.
7. Melvern, *Conspiracy to Murder*, 4.
8. Prunier, *Rwanda Crisis*, 14.
9. Gourevitch, *We Wish to Inform You*, 48.
10. Des Forges, *Leave None to Tell the Story*, 36.
11. Prunier, *Rwanda Crisis*, 6–7.
12. Gourevitch, *We Wish to Inform You*, 56.
13. Des Forges, *Leave None to Tell the Story*, 36.
14. Prunier, *Rwanda Crisis*, 11–13.
15. Des Forges, *Leave None to Tell the Story*, 34.
16. Prunier, *Rwanda Crisis*, 25.
17. Ibid., 25.
18. Ibid., 26–27.
19. Gourevitch, *We Wish to Inform You*, 56.
20. Melvern, *Conspiracy to Murder*, 5–6.
21. Prunier, *Rwanda Crisis*, 27.
22. Gourevitch, *We Wish to Inform You*, 57.
23. Prunier, *Rwanda Crisis*, 35.
24. Ibid., 27.
25. Gourevitch, *We Wish to Inform You*, 57.
26. Prunier, *Rwanda Crisis*, 28.
27. Ibid.
28. Gourevitch, *We Wish to Inform You*, 57.
29. Prunier, *Rwanda Crisis*, 33.
30. Ibid., 38.
31. Des Forges, *Leave None to Tell the Story*, 36.
32. Prunier, *Rwanda Crisis*, 39.
33. Des Forges, *Leave None to Tell the Story*, 38.
34. Prunier, *Rwanda Crisis*, 43.
35. Ibid.
36. Gourevitch, *We Wish to Inform You*, 58.
37. Prunier, *Rwanda Crisis*, 45.
38. Gourevitch, *We Wish to Inform You*, 58.
39. Ibid.
40. Prunier, *Rwanda Crisis*, 46–47.
41. Ibid., 47.
42. Gourevitch, *We Wish to Inform You*, 58.
43. Ibid., 58–59.
44. Prunier, *Rwanda Crisis*, 49.
45. Gourevitch, *We Wish to Inform You*, 59.

46. Prunier, *Rwanda Crisis*, 51.
47. Gourevitch, *We Wish to Inform You*, 59; and Prunier, *Rwanda Crisis*, 51.
48. Prunier, *Rwanda Crisis*, 53.
49. Gourevitch, *We Wish to Inform You*, 61.
50. Prunier, *Rwanda Crisis*, 58.
51. Ibid., 60.
52. Ibid., 62.
53. Gourevitch, *We Wish to Inform You*, 65.
54. Prunier, *Rwanda Crisis*, 54.
55. Ibid., 55–56.
56. Gourevitch, *We Wish to Inform You*, 64–65.
57. Prunier, *Rwanda Crisis*, 227.
58. Ibid., 67.
59. Ibid., 70–71.
60. Gourevitch, *We Wish to Inform You*, 73.
61. Prunier, *Rwanda Crisis*, 73.
62. Ibid., 93.
63. Des Forges, *Leave None to Tell the Story*, 50.
64. Prunier, *Rwanda Crisis*, 113.
65. Ibid., 113, 116–17.
66. Ibid., 174–80.
67. Ibid., 4.
68. Prunier, *Rwanda Crisis*, 4; and Des Forges, *Leave None to Tell the Story*, 31.
69. Prunier, *Rwanda Crisis*, 84.
70. Melvern, *Conspiracy to Murder*, 9–10.
71. Des Forges, *Leave None to Tell the Story*, 65.
72. Melvern, *Conspiracy to Murder*, 11–13.
73. Prunier, *Rwanda Crisis*, 85.
74. Melvern, *Conspiracy to Murder*, 14–15.
75. Prunier, *Rwanda Crisis*, 199.
76. Ibid., 200.
77. Ibid.
78. Ibid., 228.
79. Ibid., 265. Prunier estimates the number of Tutsis killed between April and July 1994 at 800,000 to 850,000 persons, with an unknown ("between 10,000 and 30,000") number of Hutu moderates killed.
80. Gourevitch, *We Wish to Inform You*, 99.
81. Prunier, *Rwanda Crisis*, 133; and Melvern, *Conspiracy to Murder*, 53.
82. Prunier, *Rwanda Crisis*, 189.
83. Des Forges, *Leave None to Tell the Story*, 89.
84. Prunier, *Rwanda Crisis*, 224; and Melvern, *Conspiracy to Murder*, 205.
85. Hatzfeld, *Machete Season*, 25.
86. Ibid., 64.
87. Gourevitch, *We Wish to Inform You*, 133.
88. Ibid., 117–18, 127.
89. Prunier, *Rwanda Crisis*, 254, 259.

90. Ibid., 257.
91. Des Forges, *Leave None to Tell the Story*, 221.
92. Prunier, *Rwanda Crisis*, 223–24.
93. Ibid., 230.
94. Melvern, *Conspiracy to Murder*, 212.
95. Hatzfeld, *Machete Season*, 10.
96. Des Forges, *Leave None to Tell the Story*, 87.
97. Prunier, *Rwanda Crisis*, 245.
98. Gourevitch, *We Wish to Inform You*, 29.
99. Des Forges, *Leave None to Tell the Story*, 131.
100. Dallaire and Beardsley, *Shake Hands with the Devil*, 75–76.
101. Des Forges, *Leave None to Tell the Story*, 132.
102. Dallaire and Beardsley, *Shake Hands with the Devil*, 229.
103. Drysdale, "Foreign Military Intervention in Somalia," 127–28, 131–32.
104. Carr, "Military Intervention during the Clinton Administration," 17.
105. Prunier, *Rwanda Crisis*, 230.
106. Carr, "Military Intervention during the Clinton Administration," 12.
107. Ibid., 235.
108. Melvern, *Conspiracy to Murder*, 231–32, 234–35.
109. Kuperman, *The Limits of Humanitarian Intervention*, 24.
110. Dallaire and Beardsley, *Shake Hands with the Devil*, 141–43.
111. Ibid., 143.
112. Des Forges, *Leave None to Tell the Story*, 595.
113. Ibid., 19.
114. Discussion Paper, 1 May 1994.
115. Des Forges, *Leave None to Tell the Story*, 622.
116. Feil, *Preventing Genocide*, 3.
117. Ibid., 7, 16.
118. Ibid., 26–27.
119. Kuperman, *The Limits of Humanitarian Intervention*, 76.
120. Ibid., 16.
121. Ibid., 76.
122. Prunier, *Rwanda Crisis*, 291.
123. Melvern, *Conspiracy to Murder*, 243.
124. Prunier, *Rwanda Crisis*, 285–93.
125. Dallaire and Beardsley, *Shake Hands with the Devil*, 423–24.
126. Wisner to Berger, 5 May 1994.
127. Tubbs, *Beyond Gunboat Diplomacy*, 18.
128. Ibid., 11.
129. Ibid.

Case Study 3

Defeating Genocide

An Operational Concept Based on the Rwandan Experience

Lt Col Keith Reeves, USAF

"Please don't kill me, I'll never be Tutsi again," were the last words of a three-year-old child after witnessing the deaths of his siblings just prior to Hutu militia slaying him also.[1] He certainly did nothing wrong, was no threat to anyone, and his death flies in the face of the basic moral fiber with which every human being is born. Yet he was merely one of more than 800,000 victims over a four-month period in a country having a pregenocide population of only 7.6 million.[2] Not only was the world unified in its shock, it was also unified in its inaction.

But Rwanda is not an isolated example in recent history—the actual numbers are staggering. Since 1945, over 60 distinct genocides have occurred with a minimum death toll of 50,000 each.[3] At the writing of this study, genocides occurring in the Sudan and Congo together had resulted in an estimated 1.25 million deaths.[4] The reason for inaction in Rwanda had less to do with apathy as much as lack of assurance of success. The world eventually recognized the genocide after initially denying it, but to no effect. According to University of Wisconsin professor Michael Barnett, the sheer scale, brutality, and apparent low-level of sophistication gave the world community an impression nothing could stop the killing.[5] Like a giant oil spill in international waters, everyone agreed someone should clean it up, but no one wanted to volunteer or knew how to go about it.

The seeds for genocide in Rwanda were planted when Belgian and German colonists placed the Tutsi minority at the top of a social hierarchy, stirring deep animosity in the Hutu majority over decades. When the Hutu came to dominate the Rwandan government shortly before independence from Belgium in 1963, these animosities spiraled into violence with thousands of deaths.[6]

In 1993 a Tutsi rebel army, the Rwandan Patriotic Front, started making significant military gains.[7] Feeling pressure from the RPF and Hutu moderates, the Rwandan government of Pres. Juvenal Habyarimana agreed to share power in a series of agreements culminating in the Arusha Accords. However, a relatively small number of Hutu remained vehemently opposed to any power sharing with the Tutsi, whom they viewed as their historical enemies, and saw elimination of the entire Tutsi people as the only and final solution.

The Rwandan genocide was a confluence of the right conditions, actors, and environment, together with international inaction, that resulted in the most efficient genocide in history.[8] A meticulously planned and skillfully executed extermination resulted in an estimated 800,000 deaths of Tutsi and Hutu moderates in 100 days. This "Rwandan killing machine" was only possible through a well-organized structure and ran nonstop until a combination of RPF victories and lack of potential victims brought it to a halt. The world community largely ignored the genocide until it was too late to save a significant number of lives. Ironically, many countries eventually contributed overwhelming support after the genocide had run its course, while a fraction of that expenditure might have averted the need.

What factors caused democracies to flout the basic laws of humanity and ignore carnage on this scale? How can militaries effectively focus their power against genocide? And, how can the international community make "never again" more than a hollow catchphrase?

Raphael Lemkin, father of the term *genocide*, defined genocide as "a coordinated plan of different actions aiming at the destruction of essential foundations of the life of national groups, with the aim of annihilating the groups themselves."[9] Prof. Benjamin Valentino further describes how genocide can include a subset of "mass killings," which also include political groups with no ethnic distinctions.[10] This paper will combine both definitions of "genocide" for simplicity.

Clearly, the best way to deal with genocide is by prevention: eliminating fuel (i.e., conflict) before it is ignited. The international community missed many opportunities to use nonmilitary instruments to encourage or coerce change. Warnings from human rights groups, intelligence analysts, and diplomats from many countries all predicted an impending ethnic clash of cataclysmic proportions prior to April 1994.[11] Appropriate nongovernmental and intergovernmental organizations should have monitored key indicators of conditions for genocide and taken appropriate actions. Military intervention was the last and least-desirable option once genocidal activity was imminent or actually occurring.

Military force can defeat genocides through an operational concept that we will call "rapid genocide intervention" (RGI). The objective of RGI is to preserve life with minimal risk while the international community takes on the more extensive task of ameliorating the conditions giving rise to genocide. RGI also defines a specific organizational structure for genocide intervention.

The Problems of Military Intervention

Military intervention to prevent or stop genocide has inherent challenges. Political will for genocide intervention is often lacking, particularly if the operation involves any risk, especially when the national interests of potential interveners are not threatened. Even if action is taken, the time required to drum up support can result in killings preventable by a more rapid response. The very concept of slaughtering humans merely because they exist is so alien to most people that until recently no conceptual frameworks have been developed to deal with genocide.[12]

Governments are reluctant to employ armed forces in foreign conflicts when their national interests are not at stake. This realism dominates the thinking of most government leaders when considering intervention. The Weinberger doctrine, penned after 241 marines were killed during peacekeeping operations in Beirut, is a clear realist statement that conflicts must threaten vital US interests before American forces are committed to combat abroad.[13]

Although not part of any official policy, this thought process influenced other administrations well after Weinberger left his post, including the Clinton administration.[14] Weinberger's perspective regarding peripheral conflicts was certainly reinforced by the unforgettable pictures of Somalis dragging the bodies of US Rangers through the streets of Mogadishu.[15] Those images poisoned American public opinion on humanitarian intervention more than the knowledge of saving thousands from famine. The same realism dominated six months later when Americans watched Rwandan death squads massacre nearly 800,000 Tutsis and Hutu moderates in 100 days.[16] The US government downplayed the slaughter to avoid questions of military intervention. World leaders, including the Clinton administration, even refused to use the word "genocide" in public for fear it would remind others of their legal obligation to act.[17] Evidence suggests this failure to classify the situation in Rwanda as genocide early on actually emboldened its perpetrators and leaders, who were sensitive to international attention and susceptible to pressure.[18]

The cold, hard fact is national interests *were not* at stake. Countries had little to gain through intervention and, potentially, much to lose. The Clinton administration predicted a backlash if America had intervened in Rwanda, with good reason, considering the fresh memories of Somalia. Even when attempting to replace this perspective with a value-driven one, the world is often thankless, or even critical.

During Operation Allied Force, despite the tens of thousands of Kosovar lives saved, a group of lawyers from several democratic countries attempted to charge NATO leaders for criminal violations of international law before the UN War Crimes Tribunal at The Hague. The charges were eventually dismissed by the tribunal.[19] And counterintuitively, Human Rights Watch was scathingly critical of Operation Allied Force and recommended severe restrictions on military intervention in the future.[20] What motivation exists for countries to replace a realist perspective with a value-driven one? In order to make military intervention in genocide a practical option, the international community should adopt systems and procedures that can overcome natural tendencies toward political realism. But even if this is accomplished, weak national will can make interventions ineffective or irrelevant.

Military intervention can commence very quickly, but reluctance to intervene in crises often results in the avoidable loss of lives during the period prior to intervention. The United Nations required six months to fully deploy its forces to Rwanda, after 800,000 had been murdered and far too late to accomplish anything except assisting the few Tutsi and Hutu moderates who remained after the RPF swept the extremist government from power.[21] This slow response had nothing to do with the lack of capability to rapidly deploy, but the lack of political will which promoted foot-dragging by the realist elements in society.[22] Even when concern over killings finally grew, the lack of a context with which to employ a rapid reaction indirectly resulted in many additional victims. By the time the public had seen the carnage on television from Rwanda and demanded action, the Hutu militia had run out of victims.[23]

Harvard professor Samantha Power points out that no US president has ever suffered for not making genocide intervention a priority.[24] The public was initially largely uninterested in the killings in Rwanda—Congress received no flood of letters or deluge of phone calls demanding action.[25] Even the media did not draw much attention to the tragedy, despite the vastness of its scope. During the genocide, 2,500 journalists converged on South Africa to report on Nelson Mandela's election, while only 15 covered the entire genocide at its peak.[26] This was largely because news editors felt the United States would never act, and therefore thought it was not very newsworthy. This created a tragic paradox: the president would only intervene if the public expressed enough anger over the killings seen in the media. But the media would only report heavily on the killings if they thought the administration might intervene.[27] However, even if the decision were made to intervene, could a conventionally trained military force actually have prevented the killing of 8,000 people a day?

The method with which most Westerners view warfare, the "Western way of war," classifies combat objectives in terms of victory or defeat accomplished in "decisive battles."[28] This context is not necessarily compatible with genocide intervention. Perceived inadequacies of the Western way of war also contribute to a reluctance to act. And if intervention occurs, the public will tend to see the defense of an entire ethnic, political, or social group as a Herculean task.

Many believe military solutions are ineffective against general uprisings within countries. Initially the State Department explained the Rwandan genocide as a spontaneous expression of tribal tensions throughout the country.[29] Genocide was thereby perceived as an extreme manifestation of riot, or violent mob action, where military capabilities would have only limited effects. Nevertheless, Lawrence College professor Nicholas Mills asserts that all modern genocides actually result from thoughtful calculations and premeditation, not sudden and spontaneous manifestations of ethnic, political, or social hatreds.[30]

Defining success in military operations driven by social values instead of national interests is difficult. Sometimes, the wrong standards are used to find victory conditions in humanitarian operations. Princeton University professor Jeffrey Herbst, and Walter Clarke, deputy chief of the US Embassy during Operation Restore Hope, state how the public did not see the Somalia intervention as a great victory even though it saved tens of thousands of lives; the public considered the United States to have "lost" when 18 soldiers were killed.

Additionally, the usual definition of war may not apply to enemy objectives. Clausewitz defined waging war as "compelling an enemy to do one's will."[31] But perpetrators of genocide do not compel their victims to do *anything*. Consider the statement of a Hezbollah spokesman, "We are not fighting so that you will offer us something. We are fighting to eliminate you."[32] The Hutu were not looking for B. H. Liddell Hart's "better state of peace" alongside the Tutsi. The political objectives, although important for a long-term solution, are irrelevant in the near and short term. Even if the Hutu had legitimate political grievances, it was the means by which they addressed them that constituted legitimate cause for intervention by the international community. This confusion over "victims" resulted in development of inappropriate and, therefore, ineffective responses to the situation in Rwanda.

Three options were considered by the United Nations for intervention: peace enforcement by "all means necessary," creating safe havens in-country, and setting up refugee camps on the borders.[33] The latter two would have saved few lives, and the first option was even worse—the United Nations was fully aware it had no plan in case the intervention force actually came into contact with the Rwandan Army.[34] A doctrine for disrupting genocides while they are occurring is needed.

Expecting countries to "step up to the plate" for the sake of humanity is not realistic. Furthermore, the formation of coalitions is a time-consuming process, where there is little unity of effort, and often results in bad decisions or critical delays. Is it possible to create a workable operational concept that is driven by values, rapidly creates decisive effects, and can be steadfast in the face of inevitable and powerful political opposition?

Rapid Genocide Intervention

Conventional militaries are structured to defeat enemies that threaten national interests. But genocide is not traditional warfare. It is a systematic process of killing a group of people simply because they exist.[35] Although stopping genocide through conventional military means is clearly possible, such as in Operation Allied Force or World War II, very high levels of political and logistical effort and large amounts of time are required to deploy the necessary forces. The time expenditure reduces the chances for saving lives. Early intervention in the progress of genocide is necessary to stop the killing.

The objective of RGI is to *quickly* and *efficiently* disrupt the process of killing while creating favorable conditions for the more difficult and time-consuming effort of addressing the underlying causes of mass murder. RGI views genocide as a system with specific critical components that can be weakened or neutralized to bring on paralysis. Once this occurs, a safe environment can exist in which local governmental, nongovernmental, and intergovernmental organizations can work to ameliorate and then eliminate the economic, political, and social conditions that led to genocide.

The characteristic which sets RGI apart from conventional intervention doctrine is the speed of employment and the limit of its objectives. The goal of RGI is paralysis of a genocide system. Any degradation in the genocidal system that leads to paralysis is a victory. RGI is the rapid disruption of genocide to preserve innocent lives while allowing time for a more conventional civil/military response to seek longer-term solutions. Since halting the killing is the immediate objective, separation of the command structures of RGI forces and the longer-term response forces is necessary. Any linking of the two will slow down the RGI response.

The genocide system that operated in Rwanda was astonishingly efficient. Less efficient genocide systems require less immediate responses to save lives. Low genocide systems may allow simultaneous deployment of RGI forces and longer-term response forces that may bring even more satisfactory results. But saving lives will always be of paramount importance.

An RGI force is intended to disrupt genocide systems. Military theorists including J. F. C. Fuller, Brig Gen William L. "Billy" Mitchell, Col John Warden, and others have developed doctrine based upon the premise that an enemy system can be paralyzed by neutralizing specific logistical, industrial, command-and-control, or other strategic "nodes." University of Massachusetts professor Ervin Staub conducted extensive research in the field of psychology to show nearly all twentieth century genocides only occurred within very obedient and hierarchical cultures, including Armenia, the Holocaust, Cambodia, as well as Rwanda.[36] Hiroshima City University professor Christian Scherrer went on to show how blind obedience to authority was especially ingrained in the culture of the Rwandan people and a significant factor in the efficiency of that genocide system. The society was similar to Stalin-era Russia with multiple organizational layers of authority and a culture of not questioning orders. The Rwandan culture of obedience went so far as to compel large numbers of priests to inform on the Tutsi members of their own congregations.[37]

To achieve a rapid halt to the killing, RGI requires timely and accurate intelligence of impending genocide. There is a critical period immediately prior to launching an efficient genocide system when the crucial warning signs are identifiable by properly trained analysts. These signs have been documented.[38]

Even efficient genocide systems tend to begin relatively slowly, and then gather momentum as their various mechanisms come up to speed. The Rwandan system began with targeted executions in the capital of Kigali before moving out into the countryside.[39] The very first victims of the Holocaust were

DEFEATING GENOCIDE

the mentally retarded, and then the process was ramped up to include Slavs, Gypsies, Jews, and others.[40] Similarly, the Cambodian genocide began with the expulsion of all the inhabitants of Phnom Penh, which initially killed the very young, the weak, and the elderly.

Obviously, the number of victims in a given time period is proportional to the genocide system's efficiency. Figure 2 illustrates how an RGI need not completely eliminate the genocide system—the goal is preservation of life while developing a safe environment for the important, if slower, international response to address long-term stability issues. *Any* reduction in efficiency of a genocide system will save a significant number of lives.

The media picked up on the primitive weapons often used in the Rwandan genocide and incorrectly deduced that its organization was equally primitive.[41] Nothing was further from the truth. The Rwandan genocide system was the epitome of an efficient killing machine. There were decisive points where

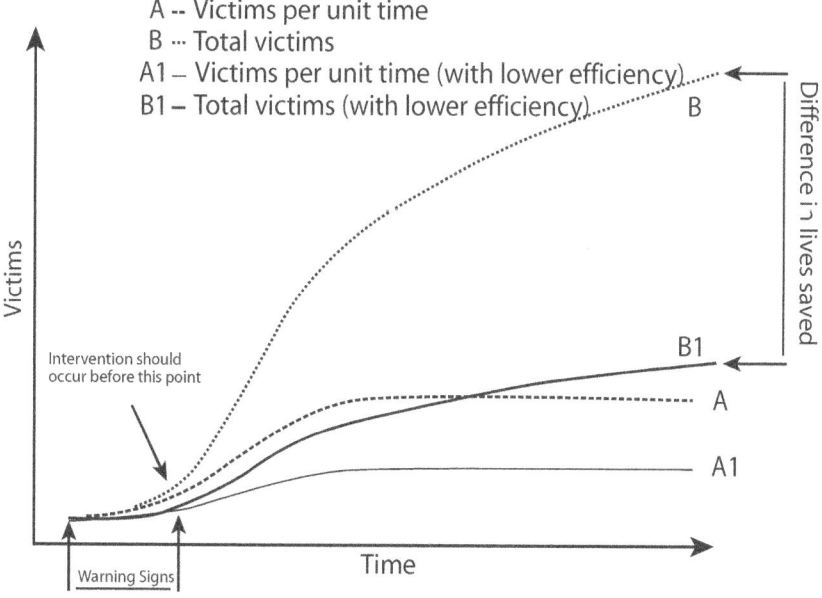

Figure 2. Graphical propagation of a genocide over time

a small, well-prepared RGI force could have disrupted the system's efficiency.

The Rwandan Killing Machine

The Rwandan killing machine was a system with multiple, interdependent layers of organization. The system was greater than the sum of its various elements. Genocides are truly dynamic systems, with each element feeding off and strengthening the others to the point where the system itself is capable of accomplishing significantly more than the various components could have if working independently. In order to implement RGI, one has to identify the components of the killing system, identify their nodes of interaction, and then target these nodes to slow down the killing process. Before turning to this nodal analysis, one has to identify the components of the genocide system. In Rwanda, these were *Akazu*, the *igitero*, the Rwandan army, the civil administration, the AMASASU, political youth groups, radio broadcasters, and the logistical infrastructure linking these elements together.

Akazu

The *Akazu* was an informal organization consisting of Hutu extremists in various high levels of government. This group was fanatical in its belief of Hutu supremacy and the necessity of eradicating the Tutsi. They had close ties with each other through blood or tribal relations, as they were mostly from the same two communes in the northwestern part of the country. Led by Juvenal Habyarimana and his wife Agathe, the *Akazu* was able to place whom they wanted in many key military and civilian positions of power.[42] These included the chief of staff of the army, several cabinet ministers, heads of key political parties, and owners of critical businesses such as public radio. Although Habyarimana's death was possibly the result (no one knows for sure) of his support for the Arusha Accords, any moderation he displayed was purely for political reasons. He was a key member and cofounder of the informal structure responsible for planning, initiating, and directing the genocide.

The total number of members of the *Akazu* is not known, but approximately 200 were captured and held under charges of crimes against humanity.[43] The *Akazu* used its influence to compel various key organizations to support their radical viewpoints. Once a government or private organization was informally under control of the *Akazu*, it became an instrument of the genocide, despite the fact that not everyone in the organization necessarily supported the killing. Passionate calls for Hutu solidarity by the *Akazu* within the various organizations, especially in light of the conflict against the RPF, made overt opposition to genocidal policies difficult for Hutu moderates.[44]

Igitero

An *igitero* (pl. *ibitero*, meaning, roughly, "attack mobs" or death squads) was at the lowest echelon of the killing machine, the tip of the spear.[45] These groups typically ranged from one to a few dozen primitively armed men. By themselves, they seemed little more than mobs armed with crude weapons and fanatical beliefs. However, their efforts were significantly multiplied by the less visible elements making up the rest of the killing machine.[46]

Rwandan Army

Although responsible for many of the early killings, the army came to provide organizational and logistical support to the genocide system that proved to be indispensable. For example, army vehicles and communications equipment provided an element of mobility, logistical support, and command and control enabling the genocide system to achieve its highest levels of efficiency.

Civil Administration

The Rwandan structure of government offered a preexisting organization that the *Akazu* could manipulate for its purposes. Rwanda is subdivided into 12 prefects (led by a prefecture), further divided into 154 communes (led by a burgomaster), and again into 1,500 sectors, 9,000 cells, and hundreds of thousands of *nyumbakumi*, which was a unit of 10 houses.[47] An appropriate level of bureaucracy supervised each layer of administration.

The formal structure this organization provided was critical to rapidly transforming a mostly peasant population into a productive pool of manpower to occupy roadblocks, accomplish searches, feed and house *ibitero*, and provide intelligence.[48] Hundreds of thousands of laborers were needed to support the lethal acts of the tens of thousands of active killers. The military and militia were too small to kill on this scale by themselves.[49] This civil administration also acted as a type of "secret police," using their authority to intimidate large numbers of Hutu that otherwise might not have participated in the genocide. It also rapidly disseminated orders, names, and addresses of targets within their administrative areas to subordinate units.[50]

AMASASU

The Rwandan government created an organization ostensibly to defend against the RPF called the AMASASU, the Alliance of Soldiers Provoked by the Age-old Deceitful Acts of the Unarists (*Alliance des Militaires Agacés par les Séculaires Actes Sournois des Unaristes* and, literally, "bullets" in a local language). They were cynically called a self-defense force but existed for no other real purpose than to antagonize the Tutsi minority. They recruited one married man between the ages of 25–40 from each *nyumbakumi*.[51] The AMASASU was the brainchild of *Akazu* members and led largely by retired military personnel. They were among the most active killers in the genocide, while the more visible Rwandan army controlled the logistics and operational plans.[52]

Political Youth Groups

Probably the most fanatical killers belonged to the two most extreme political parties, the National Revolutionary Movement for Development (*Mouvement Révolutionaire Nationale pour le Développement* or MRND) and the Coalition for the Defense of the Republic (*Coalition pour la Défense de la Republique* or CDR). These parties developed youth groups called the *Interahamwe* ("Those who stand together" or "Those who work together" or "Those who fight together") and the *Impuzamugambi* ("Those who have the same goal" or "Those who have a single goal") respectively. They were grassroots groups designed to develop pride and solidarity among the Hutu youth and were instrumental in providing highly motivated manpower to form the vicious *ibitero* that ravaged the countryside.[53] Although other youth groups existed, these two were the largest and most effective, with about 50,000 members between them.[54]

Radio

Public radio also had an enormous impact on the efficiency of the killing machine. The two main radio stations, RTML and Radio Rwanda, were used to incite, persuade, and direct large numbers of units in a rapid and positively controlled manner.[55] The privately owned RTML and government-run Radio Rwanda were both operated by the *Akazu*.[56] As an example of how the *Akazu* was linked to every aspect of government, 40 of the 50 founders of RTML were from the same commune as other members of the *Akazu*, and the daughter of the chief financier of the station was married to Habyarimana's son.[57] The radio was responsible for many tasks, including stirring ethnic tensions to incite violence, providing directions for carrying out executions, spreading fear with fictitious reports of Tutsi infiltrators, providing techniques for finding Tutsis in hiding, recalling retired soldiers to active duty, making requests for special skills such as driving bulldozers, organizing manpower for tasks such as ditch digging, demonizing moderate Hutu for not participating, and accomplishing many other functions using wit and popular programming.[58]

Communications and Logistics

In addition to these other elements, the Rwandan killing machine was held together by an intricate logistical support structure only the preexisting frameworks of the civil administration and army could provide. If the genocide was slow to develop or became out of control in a certain prefecture, the civil administration would use its network to report this information up the chain to the *Akazu*. They would then direct other prefectures to mobilize *ibitero* from the AMASASU or youth groups. The army would use its vehicles to rapidly transport the *ibitero* to where they were needed. Once there, the civil administration and army would combine to locate, isolate, identify, and kill the Tutsi. Each element of the killing machine had a specific role, and like

DEFEATING GENOCIDE

factory workers on a production line, the amount they could accomplish together was significantly greater than the sum of what they could accomplish individually. Figure 3 seeks to show how the components of the killing system interacted with one another, creating nodes of interaction vulnerable to disruption.[59]

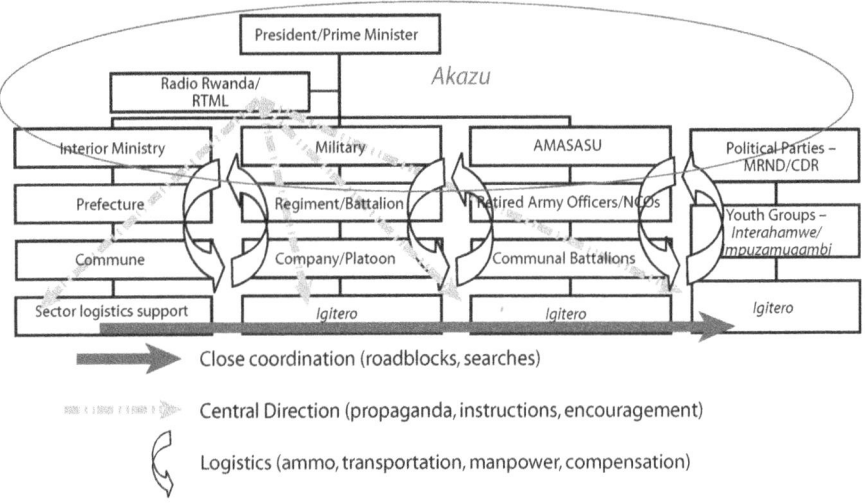

Figure 3. The Rwandan killing machine

Identifying Key Nodes

The goal of RGI is to create a significant reduction in the efficiency of the genocide at minimal risk, and thereby allow the conditions to create a long-term peace. Low-risk operations are essential because only low-risk operations have a realistic chance of gaining broad political support. Then, identification of key nodes of a genocide system is crucial to success for an intervening force.

In efficient genocides systems, these nodes will normally be located where the subsystems of a killing system interact. These subsystems include communication, logistics, propaganda, and reward subsystems.

Constant communication was required throughout the various levels of organization from the *Akazu* down to the *ibitero*. Many Tutsi were not easily distinguishable from Hutu, and the *ibitero* required help identifying them. Enormous quantities of information were needed from the local prefectures and burgomasters to identify Tutsi and find where they lived. Considering that the pregenocide Tutsi population was well over one million, the civil administration played an essential role towards the organization and efficiency of the genocide in intelligence and communications.[60] Disrupting the ability to communicate would have significantly reduced the efficiency of the genocide.

Many of the genocide participants did so only casually and were given enticements to kill. These included former Tutsi lands, cash payments, and even food. Considerable evidence suggests many of the perpetrators participated primarily because of these incentives, not for any ideological cause. Active militia membership swelled from 2,000 to 30,000, once word was spread that genocide participants were reaping huge rewards.[61] Incentives were provided through the various levels of the system. For example, a burgomaster might advertise which areas of land had recently become available to compel nonparticipating Hutu to get involved. The reward or incentive subsystem contributed to overall killing efficiency.

It is also important to note that this genocide required high numbers of "less fanatical" personnel to execute the plan. Much of the support for the genocide came from Hutus who were not fanatical but were genuinely motivated by fear and performed essential nonviolent tasks such as spying, manning roadblocks, pillaging, delivering food, and scouting. Although large in number, their low commitment would have made them easy to deter with a modest show of force.[62] Intervention forces could have significantly exploited this concept through deterrence to disrupt many areas of the genocide.

To further support this, consider the research of Yale professor Stanley Milgram. He is the psychologist famous for his experiments involving students administering what they thought were painful shocks to other participants whose false screams were heard by those directing the shocks.[63] Although none of these students were masochistic or fanatical about determining the experiment's results, they felt there was sufficient authority to justify their actions. One conclusion from Milgram's work is the most efficient way to disrupt the less-fanatical support of the genocide in Rwanda was to delegitimize the authority.

Flowing from the *Akazu* and the heads of the various organizations, central direction was required to successfully implement genocide. The impact that Rwandan radio had on the genocide's efficiency is difficult to overstate. Instructions transmitted by RTLM and Radio Rwanda would dispatch *ibitero* to concentrations of Tutsi. Propaganda was centrally directed and critical to sustaining the genocide. Fictional accounts of atrocities committed by marauding bands of Tutsi and infiltrating RPF spread fear and motivated Hutu to participate when they otherwise might not have. Operating 24 hours a day, instructions, motivation, and propaganda were transmitted to the genocide system as a whole or to individual units, as necessary.[64]

An illustration of how radio rendered the killing process more efficient can be seen in the film *Hotel Rwanda*. A convoy of 62 evacuees from the *Hôtel Mille des Collines* was attempting to reach the airport. The *Akazu* knew about the convoy and its occupants, and within a matter of minutes, Radio Rwanda directed several *ibitero* to intercept the convoy while reading the names of its evacuees over the air so the militia could separate the Tutsi when it was stopped.[65]

Additionally, the tactics of the genocide required meticulous planning at all levels to achieve the highest levels of efficiency. The genocide never would have gained its momentum with *ibitero* merely fanning out through the countryside with lists of Tutsis and their addresses. The genocide's central direction established methods that worked like a hammer and anvil. Roadblocks were placed at strategic choke points through which all had to pass. Thousands were systematically and efficiently swept up as if in a dragnet and herded to these checkpoints. The *ibitero* at the roadblocks would check identification cards and immediately execute Tutsi or those without cards. The genocide system's high level of efficiency at first gave the impression that there were very large numbers of killers, but the efficiency was really the result of meticulous planning and organization.[66]

Weapons, ammunition, and other supplies were also distributed efficiently. Although many of the *ibitero* used low-tech weapons such as machetes, even these were distributed en masse through the networks set up by existing military and civil organizations. These preexisting hierarchies had the infrastructure to handle the tens of thousands of weapons and millions of rounds of ammunition required to sustain mass murder of this magnitude.[67]

Intervention Trinity

Understanding the structure and key nodes of the Rwandan killing machine, an RGI force could have disrupted the genocide with a combination of timely intelligence, broad resolve, and rapid reaction. Timely intelligence is needed to determine when genocide is occurring—or preferably, about to occur—and how to defeat it. Resolve is necessary to decisively commit the forces without a delay, which could possibly signal tacit approval of mass murder. Rapid reaction is essential to deploy forces prior to a genocide system reaching its full potential.

An intervening force must examine the strategic situation and discern the differences between a genocide, civil war, organized crime, or just random violence. One of the major impediments to labeling the Rwandan conflict as genocide was reluctance to intervene in what many felt was merely a civil war.[68] This determination must be made quickly and decisively. This requirement, in turn, requires a corporate knowledge base of key genocide warning signs and the ability to continuously monitor them. Specific indicators of genocide are already well known. Organizations such as Human Rights Watch have monitored them for years and used them to detect the Rwandan genocide as it unfolded.[69] Once a genocide warning threshold is passed, tactical intelligence collection and analysis should go forward to identify and target key nodes for rapid genocide-system disruption.

In addition to adequate intelligence, an intervention force must enjoy the support of strong, broadly based resolve. Although it may not have completely stopped the genocide, a unified coalition could have generated significant pressure against Rwanda. Despite the warning signs leading up to April 1994, no coherent unified policy was ever implemented to influence the situation. In fact, international aid actually increased by 50 percent from 1990 to 1994 despite the escalating ethnic violence against the Tutsi throughout this time period. Christian Scherrer believes the *Akazu* members in government positions took this as tacit approval, or at least a sign of indifference by the international community.[70]

Most importantly, an RGI force must indeed react quickly. As figure 2 illustrates, a military force should intervene prior to the genocide making quantum leaps in efficiency. The level of effort required to suppress the genocide increases significantly after this point. The Rwandan genocide has shown many participants were willing to commit these atrocities when they thought it was accepted by those around them or when they simply believed others would condone it. There is strong reason to conclude even small amounts of resistance, especially by a country or organization with high international standing or power, might have deterred a large number of participants from continuing their support. Many of the poorly educated Hutu actually had a very strong conscience and understood right from wrong, but they were swept up in their culture of unquestioned trust in authority. Consequently, intervention forces could have easily dissuaded a significant number of them because of their low commitment.[71] In fact, the genocide tended to avoid areas where Tutsi put up an even *marginal* resistance.[72] Rapid reaction is all-the-more crucial in creating a deterrence factor prior to the population as a whole developing an attitude that supports or condones the violence.

An RGI force must have a standing organization to monitor and then react to situations, and it must have access to theater mobility. After warning signs of genocide start to materialize, intervention forces cannot stand up, organize, and deploy in time to create decisive effects if units are not already on a high-alert status. An intervention force must also have the ability to reach the region prior to the full mobilization of an efficient genocide system. Air mobility, including strategic, tactical, and rotary-wing airlift assets, is the only realistic means of providing needed rapid transportation. Previous failures in these areas have resulted in delays, underscoring the inability of international organizations to rapidly respond. The United Nations required a full six months for its full complement of troops to arrive, once the decision was made to deploy them. The RPF had ended the genocide already.[73]

The combination of these elements—timely intelligence, resolve, and rapid response—creates a trinity (figure 4). The absence of any of these will render the RGI force ineffective. A lack of intelligence blinds an RGI to knowing when or how to react. Lack of broad resolve will prevent access to funding and niche capabilities only wealthier countries can supply, as well as provide encouragement to the killers. Inadequate mobility will leave even the best intentioned RGI with no means to halt the genocide in its infancy.

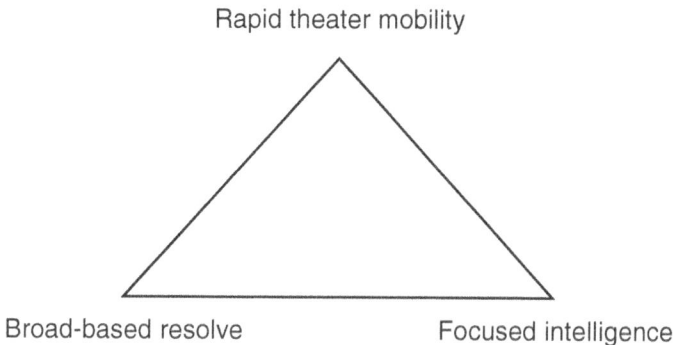

Figure 4. Intervention trinity

The Ideal Force

A well-trained force composed of regional troops lightly supported by wealthier countries could have prevented the Rwandan genocide. Shaharyar Khan, the United Nations' special representative to Rwanda, describes how such a force could have disrupted the killing if it had access to well-trained troops, plus their required logistics, engineering requirements, communications, and other support normally accompanying a rapid-reaction force.[74] He also recognized that financial constraints might prevent a full-time standing military force. However, a standing core agency at the regional level to train troops from the same general region, with a focus on RGI, is financially within the realm of possibility.

Regional standing agencies for an RGI must be able to call upon appropriate intelligence resources, regional combat power, and special capabilities, such as airlift, from wealthier countries as needed. They would maintain standing headquarters to quickly stand up and then command RGI task forces if and when mobilized. Regional combat power is essential because it can best understand the complex local cultures and customs underlying any situation. This is not an entirely new concept, considering the African Union has performed peacekeeping in Liberia, the Congo, and Sierra Leone; the Organization of American States has done the same in Haiti; and the Association of Southeast Asian Nations helped to pacify East Timor.[75]

These regional standing agencies must enjoy broad-based support yet have the power to act nearly autonomously. They need to use the cultural expertise of regional troops who can understand the underlying social conditions better and who might also have more of a vested interest in stopping a genocide in their own backyard. Additionally, these troops must have some minimum level of proficiency to give the force credibility in the eyes of the killers, as well as the organization directing them to act.

For Africa, the RGI force, centrally based in a stable country, could call upon wealthier countries to provide strategic transport and other unique capabilities such as jamming support and reconnaissance. Relatively short distance could allow high sortie rates, especially with airlift. The low-risk nature of their likely operating conditions will provide little reason for potential contributors to deny the requests.

In Rwanda, US airlift could have transported battalions of the RGI force rapidly to neighboring Zaire or Uganda. UAVs could also have deployed from nearby countries for intelligence preparation of the battlefield, while EC-130s jammed key nodes such as RTLM, Radio Rwanda, and tactical communication frequencies used by the army and civil administration to control the *ibitero*. Additionally, airpower could have targeted landline nodes to prevent backup communications between the *Akazu* and the genocide mechanisms. The EC-130s could have broadcast instructions to warn people off the streets. Not only would this have protected the Tutsis, since the largest massacres occurred when they left their homes, but UAVs could have more easily located *ibitero* traveling together in vehicles. They could have easily tracked and identified them by the weapons they carried. Precision air strikes on a few *ibitero* would have quickly sent strong messages to the others to disband and that anyone carrying weapons in large groups would die. With airpower destroying the ability of the *Akazu*, the civil administration, and the army to organize, communicate with, or support the *ibitero*, the genocide system's efficiency would have declined significantly.

But despite the tremendous capabilities airpower could have brought, the primary force would be RGI ground forces. Transported by helicopter, they could have rapidly fanned out to seize, disrupt, or destroy other key nodes of the Rwandan killing machine. They could have arrested or killed members of the *Akazu*. Their identities and probable locations would have been known from the months of intelligence previously collected by the RGI agency. RGI troops could have set up roadblocks to prevent the movement of *ibitero* and logistical support. But most importantly, the sudden presence of several thousand armed troops might have deterred the much larger number of less dedicated Hutu whose support was essential to the success of the genocide machine.

Finally, the best results of this operational concept could only result in a short-term solution. An RGI can save lives and buy time for the international community to address the longer-term issues. A full-scale campaign to remove the underlying sources of genocide (as in World War II or Kosovo) may create a longer-term solution, but the time spent creating coalitions, planning, and conducting the campaign with an objective of defeating the enemy makes preservation of life only a secondary priority.

Conclusion

Dealing with the Rwandan genocide must have seemed like trying to stop an avalanche after it had started. But with 8,000 lives being lost every day, delay was unconscionable. Despite this, the international community delayed action until after the Rwandan killing machine had nearly succeeded in its purposes.

The experience in Rwanda demonstrates that there is a real need for a new operational paradigm. A conventional intervention force takes too much time to develop and deploy. A standing RGI force could quickly disrupt genocide by making key arrests, destroying headquarters, jamming radio broadcasts, controlling the flow of materiel and personnel through roadblocks, and staging deterrent air strikes or shows of force. This would convince the less-motivated peasants, the majority of participants, that implementing genocide would be difficult and costly.

While the details of intervention were fruitlessly debated in 1994, nearly a million people died. The RGI is an immediate response with a narrowly defined goal, buying time for larger forces and preventing mass killings from escalating. Although no solution is perfect, it provides the best opportunity to turn "never again" into a meaningful phrase.

Notes

1. Des Forges, *Leave No One to Tell the Story*, 212.
2. Ibid., 15; and "Rwanda: Population."
3. Stanton, "Genocides, Politicides, and Other Mass Murder."
4. Ibid.
5. Barnett, *Eyewitness to a Genocide*, 131.
6. Des Forges, *Leave No One to Tell the Story*, 39.
7. Ibid., 4.
8. Power, "Bystanders to Genocide."
9. Valentino, *Final Solutions*, 9.
10. Ibid., 10.
11. Des Forges, *Leave No One to Tell the Story*, 142.
12. Khan, *The Shallow Graves of Rwanda*, 198.
13. "The Uses of Military Power," PBS Online and WGBH/FRONTLINE.
14. Destexhe, *Rwanda and Genocide in the Twentieth Century*, 50.
15. Khan, *The Shallow Graves of Rwanda*, 199.
16. Des Forges, *Leave No One to Tell the Story*, 15. The 800,000 number includes all deaths from general chaos of the country's internal struggles during that four-month period including Hutu moderates and soldiers from both sides. The number of Tutsi alone killed was at least 500,000.
17. Ibid., 641–42.
18. Ibid., 24.
19. Power, *A Problem from Hell*, 462.
20. Ibid. Among the recommendations were daylight bombing only, no attacks on command and control targets, no cluster munitions, more scrupulous target selection above the limits already in place, and others.
21. Khan, *The Shallow Graves of Rwanda*, 212.
22. Barnett, *Eyewitness to a Genocide*, 140.
23. Destexhe, *Rwanda and Genocide in the Twentieth Century*, 55–56.

24. Power, *A Problem from Hell*, xxi.
25. Ibid., 375–77.
26. Ibid., 374.
27. Ibid., 374–75.
28. Echevarria, *An American Way of War or Way of Battle*.
29. Barnett, *Eyewitness to a Genocide*, 133.
30. Mills and Brunner, *The New Killing Fields*, 109.
31. von Clausewitz, *On War*, 75.
32. Kilcullen, "Counter Global Insurgency."
33. Barnett, *Eyewitness to a Genocide*, 136.
34. Ibid., 140.
35. Destexhe, *Rwanda and Genocide in the Twentieth Century*, 4.
36. Mills and Brunner, *The New Killing Fields*, 108.
37. Scherrer, *Genocide and Crisis in Central Africa*, 113–14, 118.
38. An example can be found at Genocide Watch's Web site http://www.genocidewatch.org. Additionally, as of 9 February 2006, they have listed specific warning signs for genocidal conditions in Zimbabwe at http://www.genocidewatch.org/alerts/zimbabwe200202.htm.
39. Des Forges, *Leave No One to Tell the Story*, 5, 213.
40. Bergen, *War and Genocide*, 101–2.
41. Destexhe, *Rwanda and Genocide in the Twentieth Century*, 33.
42. Scherrer, *Genocide and Crisis in Central Africa*, 105.
43. Ibid., 103.
44. Ibid., 6.
45. Mironko, "Iberito." This paper was adapted from the author's dissertation entitled "Social and Political Mechanisms of Mass Murder: An Analysis of Perpetrators in the Rwandan Genocide" (Yale University, 2004). It is based upon interviews of perpetrators and victims of the genocide and deals with the meaning of the concept of *igitero* and the workings of the genocide system at its lowest level.
46. Mills and Brunner, *The New Killing Fields*, 111.
47. Scherrer, *Genocide and Crisis in Central Africa*, 108.
48. Des Forges, *Leave No One to Tell the Story*, 8, 199.
49. Ibid., 231.
50. Ibid., 10–11, 237, 262. Burgomasters held lists of known Tutsi and very specific identification procedures for determination in case of mixed ethnicity. Some were considered Tutsi if lineage was traceable back to within three generations (i.e., if a direct ancestor back to your great-grandparent was Tutsi, then so were you).
51. Ibid., 102.
52. Ibid., 5.
53. Ibid., 227.
54. Destexhe, *Rwanda and Genocide in the Twentieth Century*, 29.
55. Des Forges, *Leave No One to Tell the Story*, 10, 24.
56. Scherrer, *Genocide and Crisis in Central Africa*, 104, 107.
57. Des Forges, *Leave No One to Tell the Story*, 68.
58. Ibid., 248–50.

59. Scherrer, *Genocide and Crisis in Central Africa*, 109.
60. Ibid., 110.
61. Des Forges, *Leave No One to Tell the Story*, 227.
62. Ibid., 9–10.
63. Blass, "The Man Who Shocked the World."
64. Des Forges, *Leave No One to Tell the Story*, 6–8, 10, 24, 202, 256.
65. Mills and Brunner, *The New Killing Fields*, 118.
66. Des Forges, *Leave No One to Tell the Story*, 6, 213.
67. Ibid., 222.
68. Khan, *The Shallow Graves of Rwanda*, 196–97.
69. Destexhe, *Rwanda and Genocide in the Twentieth Century*, 91–94.
70. Scherrer, *Genocide and Crisis in Central Africa*, 179–80.
71. Mills and Brunner, *The New Killing Fields*, 112.
72. Des Forges, *Leave No One to Tell the Story*, 263.
73. Khan, *The Shallow Graves of Rwanda*, 212.
74. Ibid.
75. Ibid., 214.

Case Study 4

Côte d'Ivoire

Intervention and Prevention Responses

CDR Timothy E. Boyer, USN

"Never again," people said after the Rwandan genocide, yet it seems that all conditions will soon be in place for a similar tragedy to take place in the Ivory Coast.[1] These words were written in 2004 after four years of conflict, turmoil, and widening ethnic divides in a country once touted as "a veritable oasis of peace and stability and an 'economic miracle' in West Africa."[2] These ethnic divides have led to prejudice and discrimination that have escalated into widespread violence. If left unchecked, it is a situation that could degrade into genocide against the immigrant and Muslim segments of the population.

This study is an attempt to understand how a once peaceful and prosperous democratic country gets started down the path toward genocide by taking a look at the history of the current conflict in the Ivory Coast or the Côte d'Ivoire.[3] An analysis of factors which trigger indicators of violent conflict and genocide suggests that a high potential for genocide within the Côte d'Ivoire exists. Fortunately, international involvement has been successful in preventing genocide from developing within this West African nation.

France, the ECOWAS, and the United Nations all made significant contributions in arresting the movement towards genocide in the Côte d'Ivoire. The Côte d'Ivoire conflict serves as a case study that shows how a country acting on its own, a subregional organization, or an international organization can be effective in intervening in a crisis to prevent genocide. The international involvement in the Côte d'Ivoire conflict should serve as a model for future interventions. This case study provides potential lessons for how the United States should respond to similar situations where genocide threatens.

Background

The roots of conflict in the Côte d'Ivoire lie in ethnic, religious, and regional divides that began to surface within the country in the late 1980s. These divides, largely created by the country's ruling elite in order to maintain political power, resulted in a civil war between the largely Christian south and the mostly Muslim north. More critically, the conflict resulted in a xenophobic atmosphere which spawned ethnically based hatred and violence targeted against a large portion of the society labeled non-Ivorian.

The Côte d'Ivoire, the world's largest cocoa producer, was once hailed as the model for prosperity in West Africa. Its population represents a diversity of cultures and religion, comprised of over 60 different ethnic groups and sharing a variety of religious beliefs, with approximately 25 percent Christian, 40 percent Muslim, and 35 percent indigenous beliefs.[4] The "Ivorian miracle," a time of impressive economic growth in the 1960s and 1970s due mainly to coffee and cocoa exports, brought many immigrants into the Côte d'Ivoire, primarily from neighboring Burkina Faso, Mali, and Guinea. During these booming economic times, these immigrants were warmly welcomed into the country to provide a labor force for the cocoa plantations and elsewhere. They have come to represent more than one quarter of the country's population.[5]

Demographically, the Côte d'Ivoire can be roughly divided into northern and southern halves. Southerners are mostly Christians or adherents of local religions. The country's political elite have historically come from the South. The northern part of the country is mainly Muslim. Most of the country's wealth is concentrated in the South, where the majority of commercial development is centered. The South also contains the country's lucrative cocoa and coffee plantations, as well as the port of Abidjan, the commercial and governmental center of the nation. This port also serves as a critical hub for much of West Africa.[6] Large numbers of northern Muslims have settled in the main cities of the South and have been working the cocoa and coffee plantations for decades. In contrast to many of the surrounding African nations, the different ethnic and religious groups have coexisted peacefully for much of the nation's history.

This all began to change as the country's booming economy started to spiral downward in the 1980s and 1990s. Competition for land and resources increased, heightening tensions between the southern elites and the immigrant and mostly Muslim northerners.

When the southern elite realized that their hold on power, which they had enjoyed for over 30 years since the country gained independence, would not survive free elections, they began to disenfranchise the northerners, claiming that they were all immigrants and not true Ivorians.[7] Xenophobic ideas blossomed, and from this, the notion of *Ivoirité* was born. *Ivoirité* is a term intended to separate "real" Ivorians from immigrants or those with a "mixed" background.[8] The definition of "mixed" came to encompass Ivorians whose parents had come from other countries, and eventually most anyone in the Muslim north. The resulting political and social turmoil eventually led to a civil war between the North and South in September 2002. The situation also spawned ethnically motivated hatred and violence aimed at immigrants and northern Muslims. A UN aid coordinator summed up the situation by stating, "The Ivory Coast was where you made your dreams come true. Immigrants came here to do the jobs that Ivorian nationals didn't want to do, but now the sentiment is that non-Ivorians should be chased out of the country."[9]

History

The Côte d'Ivoire gained independence from France in 1960, and for 33 years was led by a single man, founder/president, Félix Houphouët-Boigney. Peace and stability, along with one of the most developed economies in Africa, characterized the nation for most of these three plus decades. Houphouët-Boigney's *Parti Democratique de la Côte d'Ivoire* (PDCI or Democratic Party of the Côte d'Ivoire) was the only political party allowed to exist in the republic until 1990, when economic recession and other pressures forced the government to give in to demands for a multiparty system. Despite this, Houphouët-Boigney maintained popular support and was reelected by a large margin in 1990. The period under his leadership was conspicuous for its religious and ethnic harmony. This harmony began to unravel following Houphouët-Boigney's death in 1993, when the country first began to experience the manipulation of ethnic identities by politicians faced with competitive multiparty elections and power struggles among the elite.[10]

The national assembly leader, Henri Konan Bédié, a southerner and member of the PDCI, inherited the presidency in 1993, but only after a bitter power struggle with the country's prime minister, Alassane Ouattara, who was from the Muslim North and had family roots in neighboring Burkina Faso. This power struggle ignited what was to become an escalating chain of tensions and disputes within the country, based on ethnic politics. In addition to this political power struggle, the country experienced a serious economic downturn due to falling world cocoa and coffee prices that began in the late 1980s and continued into the 1990s. Bad policies, political corruption, and the escalation of nationalistic and xenophobic ideas within the Côte d'Ivoire marked Bédié's term. He used these ideas to deflect blame for the country's continuing economic problems. It was under his leadership that the concept of *Ivoirité* was born and flourished.

Bédié fueled nationalistic currents in the prelude to the 1995 elections by instituting an electoral code that required both parents of presidential candidates to be native-born Ivorians. This code was primarily aimed at excluding Ouattara, now representing the newly formed *Rassemblement des Républicains* (RDR or Republican Rally party), from challenging Bédié for the presidency. Ouattara, who had strong support among immigrants and most of the North, was disqualified because it was claimed that his father was from the neighboring country of Burkina Faso. Bédié won the election, which was boycotted by many in the opposition due to the ethnic- and nationality-based exclusions of their candidates. Over the next several years, *Ivoirité* policies were expanded, and ethnic divides continued to widen. In 1998 land ownership was restricted to Ivorian citizens. Native southerners were encouraged to take lands that had long been held and worked by northerners and immigrants in the South.[11] Nonsoutherners were removed from positions of power in the government and military. Discontent with the government continued to grow and in December 1999, members of the Ivorian army, upset by government policies and poor pay, overthrew Bédié in a bloodless coup. Former army chief Robert Guéï, who had been fired by Bédié for refusing to use the army to crush civilians protesting the unfair 1995 elections, took over as president.[12]

President Guéï formed a government of national unity and scheduled open elections for the fall. Instead of reversing the *Ivoirité* policies of his predecessor, Guéï continued them, and the rift between the predominately Muslim North and mostly Christian South continued to grow. Guéï's government drafted a new constitution that included an article stipulating that only those born in the Côte d'Ivoire of Ivorian-born parents could stand for election.[13] This article was used to once again ban Ouattara, who now led the RDR party, from the October 2000 presidential election. The PDCI's leader and other leading candidates were barred from running as well. This effectively left Guéï to run against one candidate, the *Front Populaire Ivoirien* (FPI or Ivorian Popular Front) party's leader, Laurent Gbagbo.

When early election results indicated that Gbagbo was winning, Guéï stopped the elections, disbanded the election commission, and declared himself the winner. These actions resulted in violent demonstrations by FPI supporters and after a few days of unrest, Guéï was forced to flee to France. Gbagbo quickly declared himself president since he had received the most votes before the process was halted. Up to this point, supporters of Ouattara and the RDR were united with FPI supporters in opposing Guéï. This changed, however, as soon as Gbagbo took office and refused to schedule a new and fair election. In December 2000, RDR supporters conducted large demonstrations to protest Ouattara's exclusion from the process and demand new elections. The paramilitary gendarmery and police, along with the FPI mobs, took to the streets to stop the RDR demonstrations. This rapidly led to ethnic and religiously motivated violence, and several hundred people were killed before order was restored.[14]

In September 2002, an army mutiny led to a coup attempt against the government by former army officers. This attempted coup failed to overthrow Gbagbo, but was successful in igniting a full-scale rebellion. This rebellion split the country in two and ignited a civil war between the progovernment South and the rebel North. Rebel leaders cited the controversial elections, which excluded Ouattara, as one of the reasons for their rebellion.[15]

The rebel group *Mouvement Patriotique de Côte d'Ivoire* (MPCI or Patriotic Movement of the Côte d'Ivoire) took control of the northern half of the country and in October, signed a cease-fire agreement with the government. French forces, already in country, agreed to monitor the east-west cease-fire line. This cease-fire did little, however, to limit reprisals by government security forces in southern held areas against family members of rebel leaders or suspected opposition. Added to the security forces was the appearance of paramilitary militia groups, formed under the guise of "patriotic defense." These groups, the most extreme of which advocated cleansing the country of "immigrants," have been responsible for organizing violent riots and systematic terror against Muslim, immigrant, or northern people.[16] By November 2002, two new rebel groups emerged in the western part of the country, the *Mouvement Populaire Ivoirien du Grand Ouest* (MPIGO or Ivorian Popular Movement for the Great West) and the *Mouvement pour la Justice et la Paix* (MJP or Movement for Justice and Peace), forming a western front. Together with the MPCI in the north, these three rebel groups formed an alliance called the New Forces.[17]

In January 2003, the ECOWAS placed 1,500 peacekeepers in the Côte d'Ivoire to assist a 4,000-member French force in maintaining a cease-fire line across both fronts. Later that month, the French government brokered the Linas-Marcoussis Accord (LMA) between the country's major political parties and the New Forces. In the accord, the parties agreed to create a power-sharing, national reconciliation government that included representatives from the New Forces. They also agreed to work together on solving some of the root causes of the conflict to include modifying national identity, eligibility for citizenship, and land-ownership issues. Seydou Diarra, a native of the North and past prime minister under President Guéï, was appointed as prime minister, and in March 2003 a reconciliation government with 41 ministers was formed. The United Nations became involved in the Côte d'Ivoire situation in May 2003 with the establishment of a peace-monitoring group under the *Mission des Nations Unies en Côte d'Ivoire* (MINUCI or UN Mission in the Côte d'Ivoire). In July this government signed an "end of war" declaration, recognized President Gbagbo's authority, and vowed to implement the LMA and disarm and demobilize both state and rebel militias under a program dubbed demobilization, disarmament, and reintegration (DDR).[18]

Despite these agreements, neither side proved willing to demobilize their militias, and ethnic and political tensions continued, characterized by political deadlocks and flare-ups of ethnic related violence by both sides. The United Nations replaced MINUCI with a full peacekeeping operation under the UN Operation in the Côte d'Ivoire (UNOCI) in February 2004. In March 2004, state authorities suppressed anti-Gbagbo protests, leaving 200 people dead, and in May 2004, Gbagbo excluded three New Forces ministers from the government.[19] The Acra III agreements of July 2004 reaffirmed goals of the LMA and DDR and set new deadlines for government reform and disarmament for the fall of 2004. Both sides again failed to meet these deadlines, and in November 2004 the simmering civil war erupted again when government forces broke the cease-fire with the northern rebel forces by attempting to break through the French and UN military line separating the two sides.[20] The French military stopped the offensive and destroyed much of the small Ivorian air force after an air attack killed nine French peacekeepers. This action, in turn, ignited anti-French and anti-United Nations demonstrations in Abidjan, as well as a new round of ethnic-inspired attacks elsewhere in the South.

In April 2005, the African Union sponsored a mediation effort that resulted in the Pretoria Agreement. This agreement formally ended the civil war, further addressed demobilization, disarmament, and reintegration and the return of New Forces representation to the government, and set presidential elections for October 2005. In September 2005, President Gbagbo postponed the upcoming elections indefinitely saying a vote was impossible while the nation was divided and the rebellion still armed.[21] Herein lies a serious dilemma that is proving very difficult to resolve as the rebels refuse to disarm until Gbagbo steps aside. Some headway has been made, however, as a new prime minister and cabinet were selected for the reconciliation government in December 2005, and elections were scheduled to take place no later than 31 October 2007.[22]

Indicators of Impending Genocide

As a World Press reporter observed in January 2006, "The crisis in the Côte d'Ivoire bears a striking resemblance to events in Rwanda ten years ago. The world had better take notice."[23] Ethnic tension in a country does not necessarily equate to an impending genocide. However, factors such as ethnic polarization, xenophobic militias, government-condoned mob violence, and hate media—all fanned by a civil war—made the occurrence of genocide or mass killing in the Côte d'Ivoire highly probable. This same conclusion was expressed by observers from such expert groups as Minority Rights Group International, Genocide Watch, Prevent Genocide International, and the UN expert on genocide. This paper primarily draws upon the key indicators for genocide developed by a convention of the United Nations.

Minority Rights Group International employs a quantitative measuring system, based on current indicators from various authoritative sources, to identify groups or peoples most under threat of genocide or mass killings. In their report titled *State of the World's Minorities 2006*, the Côte d'Ivoire was ranked 11th in the world for having peoples under threat. What made the situation extremely dangerous, according to the report, is the degree of ethnic polarization within the country and the prevalence of hate speech by political militias.[24]

Genocide Watch describes genocide as an eight-stage process. At the time of the 2002 attempted coup which triggered the civil war, Genocide Watch determined that the Côte d'Ivoire was in the sixth stage of genocide, which is the preparation stage—one stage before the actual execution of genocide.[25] In his case study of the risk for genocide in the Côte d'Ivoire, written for Prevent Genocide International, Dr. Peter Stridsberg applied a genocide early warning risk model developed by the Center for International Development and Conflict Management's State Failure Task Force. Stridsberg reported that out of six possible indicators of the model, the Côte d'Ivoire "seems to have at least 3, probably 4, of these risk indicators triggered and is thus a country at risk."[26] But he also noted that even if the risk-factor analysis results are not very clear, "the presence of 150,000 militias with racist ideology, weapons training and a history of ethnic purges by common sense makes a greater threat than the little part it plays in one out of six of these indicators."[27]

In October 2005, the UN Committee on the Elimination of Racial Discrimination (CERD) published a special set of indicators that suggest increased possibilities of violent conflict and genocide. The committee warns of a potential genocide where one or more of the following 15 indicators apply:

- Lack of laws to prevent and remedy racial discrimination.
- Official denials of the existence of certain groups.
- Systematic exclusion of groups from positions of power.
- Use of identity cards indicating racial or other group identity.
- Grossly biased versions of history in school curricula.
- Forced removal of minority children for the purpose of assimilation.
- Segregation in such areas as schools and housing.
- Systematic hate speech, especially in the media.
- Racist statements by political and other leaders.
- Violence against minority groups prominent in business or government.
- Serious patterns of individual racist attacks.
- Militia or extremist groups with racist platforms.
- Large refugee flows or displacements of minority group members.
- Significant socioeconomic disparities among groups.
- Policies to block humanitarian assistance to vulnerable groups.[28]

In analyzing the crisis in the Côte d'Ivoire, several of the indicators developed by CERD seem to have been triggered to some degree. Six of these are discussed below.

Systematic Exclusion of Groups from Positions of Power

After winning the 1995 presidential election, Bédié sent several hundred supporters of opposition parties to jail. Bédié repeated this tactic in 1999 as political opposition to his rule increased, imprisoning members of the RDR, the opposition party of the Muslim North. Bédié also ensured that many potential opponents were excluded from the country's military forces. Members of the southern ethnic groups dominate the gendarmery, or national police force, as well as the government security force, the *Sûreté Nationale*.[29] Bédié sought to further exclude opponents groups from power by planning to introduce strict nationality rules before the scheduled 2000 elections that would ban both candidates and voters who had not been born in the Côte d'Ivoire.[30]

Systematic Hate Speech, Especially in the Media

The government used the media that it controls, particularly the state broadcaster, *Radiodiffusion Télévision Ivoirienne* (RTI or Ivorian Television Broadcasting), as a powerful tool in the country's ongoing crisis. In late 2004, as government forces launched attacks on rebels to the north, progovernment militia forces stormed the RTI headquarters and installed a new director there. RTI soon filled the airwaves with what was described as "calls for hatred" by the Paris-based media watchdog group, Reporters without Borders, who condemned "the fall of state media into propaganda."[31] Other reports noted that "National television and radio has been broadcasting fervent, not to say feverish, messages calling on people to take to the streets," adding that "sometimes there was a religious dimension to the speeches, which is particularly significant in a country split in two by a war that many have portrayed as a largely Christian south against the largely Muslim north."[32] The broadcasts reminded many observers of the role that Rwandan radio played in the genocide there in 1994, prompting UN special advisor on the prevention of genocide, Juan E. Mendez, to warn that "xenophobic hate speech could exacerbate already widespread violations of human rights, which in the recent past included extrajudicial killings, torture, disappearances and sexual violence."[33] In addition to using the media to convey their own messages, the government also banned or destroyed opposition newspapers in the South, as well as targeted rebel-operated radio stations in the North.

The murder of an Abidjan truck driver in November 2002, purportedly by security and pro-FPI police forces, had possible links to an article in the inflammatory state-sponsored newspaper *L'Oeil du Peuple* (*Eye of the People*). In the article, the paper published a list of people—with the driver's name among them—who had supposedly supported opposition to the government.[34]

Serious Patterns of Individual Racist Attacks

Mob violence following the October 2000 elections claimed over a hundred lives from both the FPI and RDR factions. It was after Gbagbo assumed power on October 26, however, that "state sponsored violence of the previous days intensified and developed a clear ethnic and religious focus. The primary perpetrators were paramilitary gendarmes and police. Numerous RDR supporters, primarily northern Muslims, were rounded up, tortured, and in many cases executed."[35]

The failed coup of 19 September 2002 ignited a civil war that resulted in heightened levels of violence toward immigrants and their supporters. The town of Daloa produces one-fourth of the country's cocoa and sits on the line separating the North from the South, with the population also being roughly split between ethnic lines. The town was taken over by the northern rebel forces shortly after the failed coup in 2002, with many of the ethnically Dioula youth from the Muslim North rallying behind these rebels. Government forces retook the town the next day, and within several days, as many as 100 rebel supporters were found brutally killed.[36] In Monoko-Zohi, a village west of Daloa, the bodies of 120 villagers were found in a mass grave—apparently victims of government soldiers who had gone house to house with lists of rebel sympathizers.[37]

In November 2004, Human Rights Watch reported that Muslims in Abidjan had been threatened and their houses ransacked while the police looked on.[38] The violence has also been aimed at non-African immigrants in the Côte d'Ivoire. The newspaper *Jeune Afrique L'Intelligent* (*The Intelligent Young African*) reported that in the midst of mob violence in November 2004, "there were rapes and beatings, all part of a manifest desire to humiliate the 'whites,' whoever they were—French, Belgians, British, Lebanese—and perhaps a few murders."[39]

Militia or Extremist Groups with Racist Platforms

Since 2000 the Ivorian government has increasingly relied upon progovernment militias for law enforcement, and since 2002 to combat the rebellion. Government policy has in fact encouraged civilians to form self-defense committees and participate in security tasks. These civilian militia groups have played a prominent role in perpetrating abuses against civilians in the South, with near total impunity.[40] There has also been a growth of urban tribal militias throughout the South who have access to arms and voice a violent discourse of "ethnic cleansing."[41]

Ultranationalist "patriotic youth" groups linked to the ruling FPI party of President Gbagbo have also been organized into urban militias. These groups have supported government security forces in witch hunts against members of the opposition parties and those who support them. In 2005 the *Fédération Estudiantine et Scolaire de Côte d'Ivoire* (FESCI or the Côte d'Ivoire Student Federation), a progovernment student group, committed rape and torture against students perceived to be supporting the opposition.[42]

Large Refugee Flows or Displacements of Minority Group Members

Soon after the failed coup attempt in September 2002, government security forces raided shantytowns in Abidjan, looking for weapons and rebels. The security forces burned down or demolished a number of these shantytowns, which were occupied by immigrants and Ivorians, displacing over 12,000 people.[43] According to Janine di Giovanni, a special correspondent for the *Times of London*, "the coup and the government response have displaced more than 220,000 people, and triggered a round of ethnic cleansing, largely targeted at northerners and foreigners—West Africans from other countries—who make up a quarter of the population. Shantytowns are razed. Every day, buses and planes are full of terrified residents who have lived here for generations, but cannot prove their *Ivoirité*, or ethnic purity."[44] Another figure estimates that since the beginning of the conflict 500,000 people have left the country, and another 750,000 have been displaced from their homes.[45]

Significant Socioeconomic Disparities among Groups

Most of the Côte d'Ivoire's development is in the southeast and coastal belt, so these areas enjoy greater economic advantages than the North and West. While some immigrants in the South have found work as office clerks, gardeners, cooks, and maids, the majority work as laborers in the cocoa fields.[46] Falling cocoa prices in the late 1990s strongly affected cocoa farmers.

The political and business elite of the South have benefited most economically from the civil war and have the most to lose in a democratic settlement of the crisis. Business interests are protected by both the government and the militias that support the government. Leaders of the "Young Patriots" militia groups, made up of otherwise unemployed youth, are said to receive as much as $80,000 a month from the presidential coffers.[47]

The six CERD indicators discussed above, along with the analyses of experts in the field of genocide previously mentioned, make a strong case that the Côte d'Ivoire had been and remains at risk of genocide. The main reason that this did not happened was effective and timely international intervention.

International Response

It was the popular unrest, mob violence, and eruption of civil war following the failed coup of September 2002 that finally brought an international response to the crisis in the Côte d'Ivoire. The first international responder was France, which already had a significant presence in the country, including a small military force. The French forces were soon joined by forces from the ECOWAS. Eventually the United Nations joined in the intervention efforts.

CÔTE D'IVOIRE

The Role of France

As the country's former colonial ruler, France still has significant economic interests in the Côte d'Ivoire and remains its single most important foreign partner.[48] There had been a large community of French citizens and expatriates living and working there, at least until the violence and anti-French sentiment of the last several years caused many to leave. The economic ties between the two countries, however, may be of less importance to France than the role of the Côte d'Ivoire as the linchpin of the French African commonwealth. The fear is that as the country crumbles, forcing the French who run much of its commerce to flee, "France's African commonwealth will disintegrate and with it, much that is left of France's role as a great international power."[49] Whatever the motive, France has played a major peacekeeping role in the Côte d'Ivoire since late 2002.

France was well positioned to intervene militarily, as it has had a detachment of marines garrisoned in the Côte d'Ivoire since 1961 under a mutual defense accord. Despite this, France chose not to intervene during the violence surrounding the 2000 election, aside from warning that neither it, nor the European Union would accept General Guéï's retention of power. France also rejected suggestions that it station additional troops in the country except for the purpose of protecting French nationals. This stance changed with the violence of the fall of 2002, when France sent hundreds of additional troops to augment the approximately 500 already stationed there to assist in evacuating foreign nationals and provide logistical support to government military forces.[50] The French role gradually expanded into peacekeeping and by January 2003 France had established Operation Licorne, a security force of approximately 4,000 troops. These ground forces in country are supported by air detachments consisting of 17 helicopters, which are used for both antitank and transport, and two C-160 Transall aircraft, used for transport.[51] The primary mission of Licorne has been to hold the east-west cease-fire line between government and rebel forces, preventing either side from advancing.

In November 2004, an aircraft of the Ivorian government forces bombed a French military installation in Bouaké during an offensive strike against rebel targets in the North. Nine

French peacekeeping soldiers were killed. French forces retaliated by destroying most of the small Ivorian air force on the ground. French support of the Ivorian government gradually changed to a stance of impartiality and is now perceived by many in the South as being in favor of the rebel forces. This has caused resentment, demonstrations, and violence against French expatriates and forces in the South. Any loss of effectiveness of Operation Licorne due to anti-French sentiment among portions of the population was mitigated by the arrival of West African peacekeepers from ECOWAS.

The Role of ECOWAS

In January 2003, the Economic Community of West African States placed approximately 1,500 peacekeeping troops on the ground beside the French force. The rapid deployment of the force, made up of soldiers from five African nations, marked what may have been the first time that the international community and Africans had worked together effectively in the resolution of a conflict.[52] The force, known as the ECOWAS Mission in the Côte d'Ivoire (ECOMICI), was hampered by several limitations but overall contributed significantly to the success of the peace process.

A significant limitation of the ECOMICI force was its high level of dependence on international support. France provided transport, uniforms, food, and pay. The United States provided communications equipment and vehicles, which enabled ECOMICI peacekeepers to patrol the zone of confidence that separates the rebel and government forces.[53] ECOMICI also struggled with leadership issues and did not have an effective command structure to issue directives or provide guidance.

The strength of the ECOMICI force was the fact that the West African troops shared a common background and had knowledge of the host nation. Many members of the force had visited the Côte d'Ivoire previously. ECOWAS had the human resources available to respond to the crisis and their personnel had received prior training to support peacekeeping operations. Most importantly, the impartial ECOMICI force maintained permanent liaison with belligerents on both sides. Finally, the ECOMICI troops worked well with the French forces, complementing Operation Licorne in a successful "hybrid operation." One year after ECOMICI was established, the 1,500-member peacekeeping force was absorbed into a larger UN peacekeeping operation with the establishment of the UN Operation in the Côte d'Ivoire in February 2004.[54]

The Role of the United Nations

In order to facilitate the implementation of the LMA, the United Nations established the MINUCI through Security Council Resolution 1479 of 13 May 2003. MINUCI, consisting of a 75-member military liaison group and small civilian staff, was tasked with monitoring the military situation; building trust between Ivorian government and the New Forces; and providing input on disengagement, disarmament, and demobilization. The UN military observers were deployed in the field alongside the French Licorne and ECOWAS forces, but all three of these groups continued to operate under different mandates. This posed challenges such as questions about the accountability of the Licorne force and ECOWAS shortages in manpower, equipment, and logistical support.[55]

By early 2004, it was evident that little progress had been made in implementing the LMA. In response to the continuing threat that the situation in the Côte d'Ivoire posed to peace and security in the region, the Security Council established the UNOCI by Resolution 1528 of 27 February 2004. Established under chapter 7 of the UN charter, this operation both continued and significantly expanded the functions of MINUCI, which had been essentially a political mission. It also took over from ECOMICI, rehatting the West African troops as UN peacekeepers. This UN force, which would deploy throughout the territory of the Côte d'Ivoire, would continue to work alongside French forces. Both the UN troops and the French Licorne forces were authorized to use all necessary means, including force, to carry out their mandates.

The UNOCI mission has been further developed by several additional Security Council resolutions. Resolution 1572, passed after government forces violated the cease-fire in November 2004 with ground and air offensives against rebel positions in the North, established an arms embargo for both sides and sought to stop the effects of hate media by demanding that Ivorian authorities stop radio and television broadcasting of hate messages.[56] Resolution 1609, adopted on 24 June 2005, mandated that UNOCI and French forces observe and monitor the implementation of an April 2005 joint "end of war" declaration, prevent hostile action, and investigate violations of the cease-fire. It continued with the elements for disarming and dismantling of militias of the MINUCI mandate and added: assisting a government of national reconciliation in monitoring borders, with particular attention to cross-border movement of combatants; monitoring the arms embargo; providing support for humanitarian assistance and assistance in the field of human rights; facilitating the reestablishment of a government of national reconciliation; and supporting free elections.

The UN role has been a proactive one. To combat the effects of hate radio, UN peacekeepers launched their own radio station, ONUCI FM (*Opération des Nations Unies en Côte d'Ivoire* frequency modulated radio), in August 2004. Initially available in Abidjan, the station has extended its coverage to rebel-held towns in the North.[57] In February 2006, the UN Security Council imposed sanctions against three leaders whom the United Nations deemed as posing obstacles to the peacekeeping force and sabotaging the peace process: Blé Goude, the leader of the Young Patriots; another Young Patriots leader; and a northern rebel leader who, according to the United Nations, has committed gross human rights violations.[58] The sanctions were imposed as a result of January 2006 violence aimed at United Nations peacekeepers in the country. The message being sent is that violence will not be tolerated. As of September 2006, there are over 7,000 military personnel, 900 police officers, and 800 plus civilians authorized by the UNOCI mandate.[59]

Observations

The events within the Côte d'Ivoire and the international response they have generated lead to some notable observations. The first of these is that genocide, or at least an environment that can lead to genocide, can occur even within reasonably successful states with democratic governments. The second and more important point is that the situation in the Côte d'Ivoire proves that genocide can be successfully averted through active intervention by unilateral, regional, or international entities.

For 30 years, the Côte d'Ivoire, as a state, enjoyed success, peace, and stability that were unparalleled in the region or in most of Africa. In little more than a decade, the country spiraled downwards and was on the brink of becoming a humanitarian nightmare. The root causes are fairly clear, the first being a long, slow economic decline caused by mismanagement and lack of diversification of the country's agriculture-based economy. But this alone would not be nearly enough to spawn genocide conditions. For this to occur, it took the second root cause, which was a succession of opportunistic political leaders who politicized religious and ethnic differences.[60] These leaders used the xenophobic notion of *Ivoirité* to create discriminatory policies and build ethnically based hatred among large portions of the population for the sake of maintaining their hold on power. All of this happened in a country that was still under a democratic government. While it is impossible to prove that the Côte d'Ivoire would have continued down a genocidal path, it can be said with certainty that enough warning signs existed to conclude that the country was vulnerable to and at risk of genocide.

Economic instability within the Côte d'Ivoire still exists and must be addressed. This, however, most likely will not be fully possible until the primary cause, that of the continued illegitimate hold on power by the present government is addressed. To move forward, a true representative government must be established through a free and fair electoral process.

A key enabler toward the development of genocide is the use of hate media by potential perpetrators of genocide. All media that promulgate messages of hate or incite violence against targeted groups must be curtailed. The situation in Rwanda in 1994 offers grim proof of the powerful role that media can have in the incitement and propagation of hatred and mass killing. The United Nations and regional or other international entities need to recognize when the media are being used in this role and act quickly to intervene. Hate media in the Côte d'Ivoire were addressed specifically in UN Resolution 1572, which demanded that Ivorian authorities stop all radio and television broadcasting inciting hatred, intolerance, and violence, and requested that the UNOCI strengthen its monitoring role in that regard.[61] A fundamental point to take from this is that information operations should be a key planning consideration in any genocide-related intervention effort.

The second point to be made by this case study is that a highly probable genocide was averted through an effective combination of a nation acting alone, regional or subregional organizations, and a major operation by an international organization. France, acting largely unilaterally, played a critical role in preventing genocide in the Côte d'Ivoire. The ECOMICI force represents the promising potential of the roles that subregional organizations such as ECOWAS can play in intervention efforts. The continuing success of the UNOCI demonstrates that the United Nations or other international organizations can be very effective in preventing genocide.

The quick and effective response by France in the Côte d'Ivoire crisis proved that a state acting on its own can have significant effects. France was already on the scene in the Côte d'Ivoire with a long-standing presence of French citizens, expatriates, and a small military force. Rather than abandoning the Côte d'Ivoire as tensions and violence escalated, France took a lead role in containing and resolving the conflict. The deaths of nine peacekeepers and threats and violence aimed at French citizens strengthened France's resolve rather than causing it to cut losses and leave like the Belgians did in Rwanda. The effect that French forces had was described by the French minister of defense, Michele Alliot-Marie, in a November 2004 press conference: "It is clear that, by intervening in September 2002 and in the following months, we avoided the kind of massacres that took place in Rwanda."[62] Challenges in acting unilaterally do exist. France, as a former colonial ruler with strong ties to the existing government, has had a hard time remaining impartial. When French support eventually broke from the Ivorian government to assist the peace-building process and stop humanitarian abuses, the result was a feeling of betrayal by progovernment supporters and a backlash against French peacekeepers and citizens.

The involvement by ECOWAS in the Côte d'Ivoire proves that regional or subregional bodies can be quite effective in preventing genocide. Regional organizations may be the best source of resources to monitor, mediate, and respond to crises which have the potential to develop into mass killing or genocide. To be able to do this, they must continue to develop the will, organizations, and resources to accomplish such aims. The international community needs to encourage, empower, and resource such regional and subregional organizations so that they can develop, train, and maintain crisis reaction and intervention forces. One such example is the ECOWAS rapid reaction force.

ECOWAS has agreed to establish a standby unit of 6,500 highly trained and equipped peacekeeping soldiers that can be deployed rapidly to respond to a crisis or threat to regional security. These units will be used to form a rapid-reaction task force of 1,500 soldiers who can deploy within 30 days and be augmented within 90 days by an additional 3,500 soldiers to form a peacekeeping brigade. The formation of this force, which is due to begin training this year, is a result of ECOWAS's experiences in Liberia, Sierra Leon, and the Côte d'Ivoire.[63]

The Côte d'Ivoire example also proves that an international organization can be highly effective in preventing genocide. After demonstrating an inability or unwillingness to intervene in Rwanda and other places, the United Nations finally proved that it can be effective in preventing genocide through the UNOCI. The UNOCI is an example of how successful a UN operation can be when given the right direction and resources by a cooperative and determined Security Council. The UNOCI is "part of an emerging trend in UN peacekeeping in which the UN force is actually a hybrid of two or three different peace operations that are subsumed under—or operate in tandem with—the United Nations. Three key words underline the UNOCI mission. These are transformation [of the ECOWAS forces], absorption [of MINUCI], and cohabitation [with the French forces]. The success of the UNOCI mission will depend on how well these three factors play out."[64] The United Nations and other international bodies such as NATO will hopefully use the success of the UNOCI as a model from which to build upon for future interventions in other conflicts.

The UNOCI is a good indication of the significant progress that the United Nations has made since the events in Rwanda in 1994 toward responding to situations that are heading towards genocide. Another notable step has been Sec-Gen Kofi

Annan's designation of a UN special adviser on the prevention of genocide in July 2004. Juan E. Mendez was appointed to the role, which is to "act as an early-warning mechanism to the Secretary-General and the Security Council about potential situations that could develop into genocide, and to make recommendations to the Council about how the United Nations can prevent these events."[65]

Implications for Future US Intervention

The United States played a small role in the intervention in the Côte d'Ivoire. This is not to say that the United States should not learn from these events and be prepared to act in future, similar situations. As the world's sole superpower, the United States wields considerable influence, power, and resources to help in identifying and preventing genocides. The 2006 *National Security Strategy* specifically addresses the need to ensure intervention in such instances and recognizes the important role that the nation plays, stating, "It is a moral imperative that states take action to prevent and punish genocide. History teaches that sometimes other states will not act unless America does its part."[66]

This is not to say that the United States should feel an obligation to commit military forces to every conflict that has the potential for genocide. The United States can generate considerable effects without placing US peacekeepers in harm's way by using political, diplomatic, and economic instruments to either influence the root causes or pressure the groups or governments responsible for promoting genocide. The United States should use its muscle in the UN Security Council to ensure that conflicts that show even the most preliminary indicators of a genocide or mass killing get the attention and intervention necessary to diffuse the situation and protect groups at risk.

The root causes and enablers of these type conflicts must be identified and addressed. Without removing these causes, intervention will likely remain primarily a peacekeeping effort. In the Côte d'Ivoire situation, economic factors played a large role in the development of a situation that could easily lead to genocide. The United States can use its economic and informational tools to help restore the economies of countries such as the

Côte d'Ivoire through assistance programs and development of new US markets. In addition to helping a state in crisis regain its own stability, the United States can and should make such efforts as supplying funds and other resources to the international or subregional actors that can effectively intervene. Shortly after ECOWAS forces deployed to the Côte d'Ivoire, the United States contributed $1.5 million in contractor and logistical support. This support was primarily in the areas of communication and transportation and included trucks, jeeps, and other vehicles.[67] At a relatively small cost, the US government was able to provide a significant increase in transportation and communication resources available to the West African peacekeeping force. Another major resource that the United States can provide is airpower.

Joint or Air Force doctrine does not specifically address intervention in genocide-related conflicts. Missions under the umbrellas of crisis response, peace enforcement, or foreign humanitarian assistance are close enough to be applicable. Air Force support capabilities for such missions, as listed in Joint Publication (JP) 3-07.3, include airlift; intelligence, surveillance, and reconnaissance; command and control of air operations; communications and information gathering; aerial refueling; personnel recovery; air traffic control support; joint fire support; combat air patrol; airspace control; early warning of hostile actions; delivery of humanitarian aid; aeromedical evacuation; deterrence of hostile actions; protection; logistics; and resupply.[68]

A primary area in which US airpower can contribute is by providing logistical and air mobility support to troop-contributing nations. A large constraint affecting the capabilities of the ECOWAS force responding to the Côte d'Ivoire or other West African crises was the lack of air transport, which is virtually nil within the armed forces of the region.[69] The United States can fill this critical void by supplying air assets or training and equipping regional forces.

US air and space assets can provide critical ISR capability to help recognize acts and identify conditions leading to genocide. Potential perpetrators of humanitarian abuses might be dissuaded if they know that they are being monitored from above. Air assets can be used in information operations to warn potential victims, dissuade perpetrators, or counter hate media. Should deterrence measures fail, tactical aircraft could be used for precision strikes to disrupt those who are perpetrating violence.

Finally, the United States and other leading nations within the international community should continue to encourage and assist in the development of regional or subregional crisis response capabilities. Security and defense policies, such as France's *renforcement des capacites Africaines de maintien de la paix* (RECAMP or reinforcement of African peacekeeping capabilities) and the US government's Africa contingency operations training assistance (or ACOTA) program, will help African states, under the umbrella of subregional organizations to acquire military capabilities to help them conduct peacekeeping operations.[70]

Conclusion

The 2002–03 crisis in the Côte d'Ivoire exhibited numerous indicators that warned of a high potential for genocidal violence. Fortunately, intervention efforts by France, ECOWAS, and the United Nations were both timely and effective in preventing such an occurrence. Operations within the Côte d'Ivoire should serve as model from which to build for future international intervention efforts.

From Kosovo to Rwanda to the Sudan, the pledge of "'never again' has turned into 'again and again.' Again and again, the response to genocide has been too little too late."[71] No longer can the world afford to allow genocides to unfold by either turning a collective blind eye, or choosing not to act in a timely manner. Because the causes of genocides vary widely, and fully predicting the occurrence of such may be impossible, early warning signs should be heeded with the worst case assumed. When such situations arise, the international community should respond quickly, decisively, and effectively. Such involvement can be accomplished unilaterally, by international organizations such as NATO or the United Nations, or by regional or subregional bodies. As seen in the Côte d'Ivoire, the most successful interventions will likely require a combination of these means.

Notes

1. Gregston, "Rwanda Syndrome on the Ivory Coast."
2. *Jane's SENTINEL Security Assessment: West Africa*, 125.
3. While many English language sources persist on using the name Ivory Coast, since 1986 the Côte d'Ivoire has requested that the French form of the country's name be used in all languages. The author will therefore use the Côte d'Ivoire except in quotations.
4. International Crisis Group, "Conflict History." Figures for the distribution of religions vary by source. Jane's figures are: 22 percent Catholic, 5.5 percent Protestant (27.5 percent Christian), 38 percent Muslim, 17 percent Animist, and 17.5 percent other. *Jane's SENTINEL Security Assessment: West Africa*, 120.
5. International Crisis Group, "Conflict History."
6. Chirot, "Chaos in Ivory Coast."
7. Ibid., 2.
8. Stridsberg, "Cote d'Ivoire, Historical Background."
9. Thibodeaux, "Ivory Coast Fears a Wider War."
10. *Jane's SENTINEL Security Assessment: West Africa*, 106.
11. Chirot, "Chaos in Ivory Coast."
12. Gberie and Addo, *Challenges of Peace Implementation in Cote d'Ivoire*.
13. International Crisis Group, "Conflict History."
14. Human Rights Watch, "Cote d'Ivoire."
15. Gberie and Addo, *Challenges of Peace Implementation in Cote d'Ivoire*.
16. Stridsberg, "Cote d'Ivoire, Historical Background."
17. Bureau of African Affairs, "Background Note."
18. Ibid.
19. International Crisis Group, "Conflict History."
20. Chirot, "Chaos in Ivory Coast."
21. Merrill, "Citizen Soldiers."
22. *UN Security Council Resolution (UNSCR) 1721*.
23. Gregston, "Rwanda Syndrome on the Ivory Coast."
24. Lattimer, "Peoples under Threat," 12–13.
25. Stridsberg, "Cote d'Ivoire, Historical Background."
26. Ibid. Stridsberg says that this model, presented at the Stockholm International Forum 2004, is perhaps the most successful genocide early warning system so far, successfully predicting 79 percent of historical genocide based on a risk factor analysis. Information on the model can be found in Goldstone, *State Failure Task Force Report*. http://www.cidcm.umd.edu/publications/papers/SFTF%20Phase%20III%20Report%20Final.pdf.
27. Stridsberg, "Cote d'Ivoire, Historical Background."
28. United Nations, "Decision on Follow-up to the Declaration on the Prevention of Genocide."
29. "Cote d'Ivoire Country Report," 10.
30. "Conflict Country Briefings: Cote d'Ivoire," *European Defense*, 5.
31. British Broadcasting Corporation, "Country Profile: Ivory Coast."
32. Gregston, "Rwanda Syndrome on the Ivory Coast."

33. Ibid.
34. di Giovanni, "Terror and Ethnic Cleansing in Ivory Coast."
35. Human Rights Watch, "Cote d'Ivoire: The Human Rights Costs."
36. di Giovanni, "Terror and Ethnic Cleansing in Ivory Coast."4.
37. "Crisis in Cote d'Ivoire," *Genocide Watch*.
38. Gregston, "Rwanda Syndrome on the Ivory Coast."
39. Ibid.
40. Human Rights Watch, "Cote d'Ivoire."
41. International Crisis Group, "Côte d'Ivoire: The War Is Not Yet Over."
42. Human Rights Watch, "Cote d'Ivoire."
43. Bureau of African Affairs, "Background Note."
44. di Giovanni, "Terror and Ethnic Cleansing in Ivory Coast."
45. Stridsberg, "Cote d'Ivoire, Historical Background."
46. Thibodeaux, "Ivory Coast Fears a Wider War."
47. International Crisis Group, "Cote d'Ivoire: No Peace in Sight."
48. Bureau of African Affairs, "Background Note."
49. Chirot, "Chaos in Ivory Coast."
50. Ibid.
51. "Conflict Country Briefings: Cote d'Ivoire," *European Defense*, 4.
52. Itano, "Next Door, Lessons for Liberia."
53. Ibid.
54. Gberie and Addo, *Challenges of Peace Implementation in Cote d'Ivoire*.
55. Ibid.
56. UNOCI, "Côte d'Ivoire-UNOCI-Mandate."
57. British Broadcasting Corporation, "Country Profile: Ivory Coast."
58. Bax, "Too Little, too late? UN Sanctions in Ivory Coast."
59. UNOCI, "Facts and Figures."
60. Statement of Timothy Docking, PhD.
61. UNSCR 1572.
62. Gregston, "Rwanda Syndrome on the Ivory Coast."
63. "ECOWAS [Economic Community of West African States] 'Rapid Reaction Force,'" *Africa Research Bulletin*.
64. Gberie and Addo, *Challenges of Peace Implementation in Cote d'Ivoire*.
65. United Nations. "Annan Chooses Former Political Prisoner."
66. The White House, *National Security Strategy of the United States*, 2006.
67. Statement of the Honorable Walter H. Kansteiner III.
68. Joint Doctrine Publication 3-07.3 *Peace Operations*, Figure II-2 Air Support Capabilities, II-4.
69. "ECOWAS [Economic Community of West African States] 'Rapid Reaction Force,'" *Africa Research Bulletin*.
70. Ibid.
71. "The International Campaign to End Genocide," *GenocideWatch.org*.

Conclusion

Dr. Douglas C. Peifer

Genocide scholars, journalists, and activists have contributed substantially to understanding the causes and conduct of genocide and to alerting the public and policy makers of potential and ongoing genocidal crises. Where they have fallen short is in providing concrete, operational advice on how intervention forces can stop mass killing and what sort of capabilities intervening forces must have in order to accomplish that mission. Those tasked with stopping genocide soon discover that no doctrine exists for genocide intervention, since genocide intervention falls neither in the realm of peacekeeping nor within the realm of war fighting. Models, recommendations, and best practices for uncontested humanitarian interventions and peacekeeping are not useful as guides to stopping the deliberate, organized killing of one group by another. War-fighting doctrines are unsuitable because intervening forces, whether UN, regional, or US, seek to avoid becoming belligerents if possible. Support for intervention missions will be extremely limited if put in terms of making war for humanitarian purposes. The closest framework is the concept of "peace-enforcement operations." Even here, doctrinal guidance is unhelpful, if not misleading. The JP 3-07.3, *Peace Operations*, maintains that peace operation forces (termed PO forces in the joint publication) must still act impartially even when conducting peace-enforcement operations. The publication blandly instructs intervening forces to restore order and forcibly separate belligerent parties while using restraint and minimum force. How this is to be done remains unclear. Military commanders must anticipate that genocide-intervention missions will pose particular challenges in that intervention forces should not treat killers and victims impartially. Furthermore, restoring order may involve removing civil authorities rather than supporting and reinstating them, as suggested by JP 3-07.3.

The preceding case studies provide a sense of the challenges and possibilities for genocide-intervention missions, drawing upon specific historical examples rather than contrived generic scenarios or the ongoing, evolving emergency in Darfur. Each case study seeks to provide a sense of specific context, with the first study focusing on Somalia in 1992–93, the second and third, Rwanda during the spring of 1994, and the last, the Côte d'Ivoire during the period 2002–05. The case studies provide overviews of the causes, conduct, and contours of genocide within these particular settings, with specific analyses as to whether and how intervention might have been more effective. In each case, the authors caution that prevention is preferable to intervention, but assert that *if* intervention becomes necessary, airpower can contribute to mission success.

Aaron Steffens provides a set of strategic and operational lessons for intervention operations based on his analysis of UNOSOM, UNITAF, and UNISOM II missions in Somalia in the early 1990s. At the strategic level, Steffens argues that prevention would have been much less costly than intervention and that there were at least three clear opportunities "prior to the formation of UNOSOM I where US leadership and UN involvement might have mitigated the Somali crisis." He argues that early intervention is always better than crisis intervention and notes that setting time limits to these missions, while popular with both the public and military desirous of clear "exit strategies," can undermine the prospects for success.

At the operational level, Steffens cautions that in complex contingency operations, one cannot artificially separate humanitarian intervention from nation building. In Somalia famine and mass starvation could not be addressed merely by airlifting food and supplies into the country. The deliberate manipulation of food supplies by militias and clan factions had to be stopped. Steffens argues that nation building, in the forms of political reconstruction, demobilization, and disarmament, was a precondition for success. Even at the operational level, there is need to tightly integrate and unify diplomatic, military, and humanitarian efforts.

This will prove challenging. Steffens and the other authors recommend that regional organizations provide the manpower for intervention efforts, with the US focusing on airlift and logistical support. As for the utility of coercive airpower, Steffens issues a warning: in Somalia, the use of AC-130 gunships "signaled a departure from coercion to blunt-force attack, and it represented a declaration of war."

George Stanley and Keith Reeves examine the failure to intervene in Rwanda in 1994 and provide assessments of whether and how intervention might have prevented genocide. Stanley notes that a Carnegie Commission panel concluded that "a modern force of 5000 troops, drawn primarily from a single contributing country, and inserted between April 7th and 21st could have significantly altered the outcome."[1] While not contesting this assessment, Stanley notes that the risk level would not have been low, and that military planners could not have assumed a passive environment for intervention. The French intervention operation of summer 1994 (Operation Turquoise) encountered little opposition in part because it avoided injecting French troops into the maelstrom of an ongoing genocide, and did more to assuage the moral sensibilities of the French public after the genocide had run its course than it did to stop the killings.

While warning that intervention carried more risk than many contend and echoing Alan Kuperman's contention that a 7–21 April intervention time frame was unrealistic, Stanley asserts that "any intervention would have likely saved thousands of Tutsi lives." Had the political will existed, an intervention might have been possible, with airpower playing a central role. Rapid intervention hinges on airlift, and only a few nations possess the sort of strategic airlift that would have enabled rapid intervention. Yet beyond airlift, airpower could have played an important role in impeding the Rwandan genocide. Stanley notes that RTL radio played a key role in instigating and guiding Rwanda's killers. Its broadcasts could have been disrupted by deploying an EC-130 Commando Solo aircraft, clearly sending a signal that genocide would not be tolerated and complicating the efforts of the genocidaires. Furthermore, reconnaissance aircraft could have been deployed to locate roadblocks and disseminate warnings. While not available at that time, the MQ-1 Predator now provides the reconnaissance capabilities that can be deployed into nonpassive environments without risk to intervening or monitoring forces. As a last resort, Stanley notes that aircraft could have been used to directly attack roadblocks manned by militias, though collateral damage in the form of civilian casualties would have been the price of directly applying firepower to dismantle checkpoints.

Keith Reeves applies airpower theory to examine genocide as a system, to identify the system's critical vulnerabilities and connections, and to construct a model for rapid genocide intervention or RGI. Much as students and instructors at the Air Corps Tactical School in the 1930s sought to uncover the vulnerabilities of modern warfare by examining the industrial web that generated and supported it, so Reeves seeks to find the organizational connections that sustain genocide. He argues that the Rwandan genocide, far from being a primitive, spontaneous, and poorly orchestrated expression of hate, was instead a complex, highly organized effort sustained by a network connecting political actors, civil authorities, the Rwandan armed forces, and militias such as the *interahamwe* and *impuzamugambi*. Applying more recent airpower theory that postulates that one can cause the strategic paralysis of an enemy by applying rapid, simultaneous, and parallel attacks on the components of the enemy's military system, Reeves argues that one should consider this approach to genocide. His concept of RGI envisions disrupting ongoing genocide by targeting the connections between the supporting components of the genocide machinery. Reeves notes that disrupting genocide is only an interim solution, but argues that a rapid, short-term response buys time and saves lives so that longer-term responses can be generated.

Reeves' concept of rapid genocide intervention rests on three pillars: broad resolve, timely intelligence, and rapid reaction. In keeping with the book's focus on operational responses, Reeves provides little detail about how to generate the sort of broad international resolve necessary for rapid, timely, and effective responses to genocide. Instead, he focuses on the other two elements of RGI, timely intelligence and rapid reaction. Reeves notes that at the strategic level, nongovernmental organizations such as Human Rights Watch and Genocide Watch already are providing alerts, watches, and warnings of impending mass killings. National and international agencies can act on these alerts and gather additional assessments of conditions on the ground. At the operational level, Reeves notes that reconnaissance aircraft and UAVs could provide more detailed information, monitoring conditions, and providing timely intelligence of where and how mass killings are taking place. The third element of his concept, rapid reaction, rests on airlift and air mobility. Reeves' ideal force for RGI would be regional in composition, with the United States and/or NATO providing air assets ranging from strategic and tactical airlift assets to helicopters and reconnaissance craft to UAVs.

The final case study of the volume, Timothy Boyer's examination of the Côte d'Ivoire during the period 2002–05, analyzes a case of successful genocide prevention. Boyer notes that by 2002, the Côte d'Ivoire was at stage six (preparation) of the Stanton genocide model. The Ivorian state showed numerous signs of impending failure and exhibited almost all CERD indicators of potential genocide. According to Boyer, "A highly probable genocide was averted through an effective combination of a nation acting unilaterally [France], regional or subregional organizations [ECOWAS], and a major operation by an international organization [UNOCI]." While less theoretical than Reeves' case study, Boyer provides an example of the sort of assets and capabilities that stopped an impending genocide. The French intervention (Operation Licorne) was fairly robust, consisting of some 4,000 troops, an air detachment of 17 helicopters, and two C-160 Transall aircraft. Most interestingly, UNOCI set up its own radio station so it could communicate the mission of its 8,000 uniformed personnel directly to the local population.

Boyer concludes that Operation Licorne and regional and international intervention efforts provide valuable models for addressing the threat of imminent genocide. While direct US involvement was minimal, US diplomatic and economic support of ECOWAS and later UNOCI forces was important, helping to fund trucks, jeeps, and communication equipment. French airpower, both in the form of airlift and in the form of helicopters, served as a vital enabler of Operation Licorne, with the French mission working closely with UNOCI in damping down violence.

The case studies show that specific context matters and caution that prevention is less costly and more effective than intervention. Yet in seeking operational solutions to stopping ongoing mass killings, each case study posits that airpower might have played a valuable role beyond simply transporting and sustaining peacekeeping troops. Given that the US Air Force has devoted little thought to genocide intervention, perhaps it is fitting to summarize and explore airpower's capabilities in this realm. Airpower alone cannot stop ongoing genocides, but it can support and assist intervention efforts in ways overlooked. This is especially important in that the US public has a limited appetite for sustained nation building, and the notion of deploying significant numbers of US ground troops to Darfur, the Congo, and other crises areas is unrealistic given current overstretch and competing commitments in Iraq and Afghanistan. Rather than focusing on operational responses that call for US "boots on the ground," a better US strategy for genocide intervention would be to support regional or UN forces through the small US expeditionary forces providing key enabling capabilities. Regional and UN peace-enforcement missions tend to be weakest precisely in those areas where the United States and its Air Force excel: strategic airlift and theater mobility, communications, ISR, medical evacuation (MEDEVAC) and emergency care, radio suppression and broadcasting, and (as a last resort) coercive airpower.

The US Air Force already has the organizational construct to provide an expeditionary force that could support and assist regional or UN intervention ground forces engaged in genocide intervention and peace enforcement. In 1998 then chief of staff of the US Air Force, Gen Michael Ryan, and acting secretary of the Air Force, F. Whitten Peters, launched a reorganization of the Air Force for the very purpose of generating enhanced capability to deploy and sustain air and space expeditionary task forces (AETF). These task forces, ranging in size from wings to groups to squadrons, each have built-in command, control, and staff support structures and are fully tailorable forces.[2] The Air Force has emphasized that all personnel and assets should fall within the framework of this expeditionary construct. While task forces deployed to Iraq and Afghanistan have focused on supporting US, NATO, and coalition war fighters, the concept of organizing an AETF with the sort of capabilities that lend themselves to supporting non-US regional forces or UN operations is entirely reasonable.

Devising genocide intervention strategies and operational concepts will be highly contextual. The concept of safe havens, for example, was appropriate for Kurdish Iraq, problematic in Bosnia, and inappropriate in Rwanda, where Tutsis intermingled with Hutus and roadblocks impeded movement.[3] Likewise, imposing "no-fly zones" depends on local conditions: a no-fly zone might have protected Shiites in southern Iraq from Saddam's ruthless post–Desert Storm subjugation campaign in which Iraqi helicopters played a crucial role, yet even a massive Allied air presence over Kosovo in 1999 could not stop Serbian ground forces from terrorizing and expelling Kosovar civilians. Rather than focusing on devising detailed operational plans for stopping genocide, the United States should focus on developing small expeditionary task forces that provide regional and international organizations with capabilities they sorely lack. Some of these key capabilities follow.

Strategic and Theater Air Mobility and Airlift Support

The US Air Force clearly understands the importance of strategic airlift in genocide intervention operations and already directly contributes to African Union operations in Darfur by transporting and supplying various contingents. Since 2003, for example, the 786th Expeditionary Squadron operating out of Ramstein Air Base, Germany, has conducted seven missions transporting Rwandan contingents into the region. Its C-130s, along with C-17s from Charleston AFB, South Carolina, have provided the essential strategic airlift underpinning the operation, with Air Force personnel also contributing to airfield operations.[4] Yet strategic airlift is only part of the equation. Intervention forces, once transported into the region, often lack theater mobility. The UN African Union Mission in Darfur (UNAMID), which replaced the African Union's only operation in Darfur in early 2008, has faced great difficulties in finding donor nations willing to supply helicopters and tactical airlift assets. UN secretary general Ban Ki-moon commented in January 2008 that "In the past weeks and months, I have contacted, personally, every possible contributor of helicopters—in the Americas, in Europe, in Asia. And yet, not one helicopter has been made available yet."[5] Ban Ki-moon attributed the difficulty of finding donors to "lack of political will," with unnamed diplomats at the United Nations elaborating that "past attacks on helicopters" have dampened the enthusiasm of donor nations loathe to put their valuable aviation assets at risk. In short, the United Nations understands the need for theater mobility. It simply cannot find countries willing to contribute to filling this vacuum.

The US Air Force, which has staked the claim to be the leading service in airpower (not simply US Air Force) thought, should move beyond simply patting itself on the back for supplying the indispensable long-range airlift that underpins many crisis-intervention operations. Building on the mechanism of the AETF, it should cobble together an expeditionary task force that provides ground-centric UN or regional peace makers with theater and tactical air mobility as well. This may well entail drawing in US Army and US Marine Corps components, with a joint expeditionary airlift package conceivably including Air Force C-130s, Army CH-47 transportation helicopters, and Marine Corps MV-22 Osprey tilt-wing rotor aircraft. The numbers required would be limited: UNAMID, currently slated to become one of the largest UN missions to date, desperately seeks 24 helicopters. Operation Licorne, the French intervention effort in the Côte d'Ivoire, supported its substantial ground forces with an initial aviation contingent consisting of

> a single Fennec light helicopter, which was reinforced by two SA.330 Cougars [helicopters originally developed by *Sud Aviation* called Pumas if assembled by Westland Helicopters] of the COS (*Commandement des Opérations Spéciales* [or French Special Operations Command]), and a Transall C.160 of ET 2.64 [*Escadrille de Transport, Armée l'Air*, or French Air Force Transport Squadron]. . . . another Transall, four Gazelles [Another *Sud Aviation*–developed helicopter] from the 5 RHC [*Régiment d'Hélicoptères de Combat, Aviation Légère de L'Armée de Terre*, or French Army Aviation Combat Helicopter Regiment] and two Pumas were added subsequently.[6]

Communications Support

While the US Air Force can and should take the lead in providing airlift and mobility to peacemaking forces, it can contribute in many other ways, with communication support leading the way. UN and regional forces often are poorly equipped with communication gear and support and at times are dependent on contractor support which may evaporate if the situation becomes dangerous. This is no indictment of private contractor support, but contractors who have signed up to support peacekeeping and monitoring missions may be unprepared for peace enforcement. Lt Gen Roméo Dallaire, recalling the communications capability of his small UNAMIR force, wrote that "It was difficult to get messages to troops in the field . . . . Getting messages to headquarters was equally difficult. They either had to be hand delivered—a problem when both fuel and vehicles were at a premium—or relayed over our radio network. Unfortunately, our Motorola radios (unlike those carried by both the RPF and the RGF) had no encryption capability."[7] As for communicating with UN Headquarters, Dallaire depended on contractor support to operate and maintain his satellite communications. Luckily for him, six of his civilian communications staff "had insisted on staying with [UNAMIR] after the rest of their colleagues had been evacuated," even though "they were living in squalor."[8] A small AETF that could provide robust, secure, and dependable communications and support personnel to regional and UN commanders engaged in genocide-intervention missions would be immensely valuable.

ISR Support

The US Air Force excels at providing timely operational ISR support to ground commanders, a capability that many regional and international organizations sorely lack. UN and regional peacekeepers operate largely in the dark once observation posts are overrun and established separation lines are ignored. The Dutch commander in charge of the southern sector of the Srebrenica safe zone in 1995, for example, had to send out one of his armored personnel carriers "to find the enclave's new front line" once Serbs rolled past his observation posts.[9] More recently, an African Union observation mission in Darfur was overrun by rebel forces on 30 September 2007, suffering 10 dead, 10 wounded, and 30 missing in action. The lightly equipped African Union forces apparently had no idea of the size or strength of rebel groups forming in the area.[10] The US Air Force certainly could support intervention missions by sharing satellite imagery, by launching reconnaissance aircraft, or by deploying the sophisticated Global Hawk RQ-4 UAV. This support would be costly and contested, given concurrent demands in Iraq, Afghanistan, and elsewhere. Far more useful would be less costly, lower-tech ISR assets, such as the Army's tactical Hunter or Raven UAVs. Furthermore, considering that the likelihood of genocide is high in many areas of the world where the main challenge to reconnaissance and observation craft comes from man-portable air defense system (MANPADS) missiles, the Air Force should consider the utility of substituting disposable, high-altitude observation balloons for scarce satellite imagery. Rather than thinking in terms of US "boots on the ground" in crisis areas such as Darfur, Somalia, and the Congo, the US should support regional and international forces by providing them with ISR capabilities so that reconnaissance rests on more than lightly armed troops in a jeep.

MEDEVAC and Field Hospital Support

One of the key challenges to intervention forces embarked on peace-enforcement operations is providing emergency care and timely medical evacuation to peace enforcers. While blue helmet peacekeepers can claim that both sides have acknowledged their special neutral status and therefore are obliged to assist in evacuating injured personnel, forces intervening to stop genocide must recognize that they have taken sides and may well be the target of those whose genocidal campaign they intend to thwart. Indeed, those groups conducting genocide may specifically target intervening forces in order to demoralize them, stun them into passivity, or convince the populace of the contributing country to withdraw their forces. This certainly was the case in Rwanda, with Hutu extremists intentionally targeting Belgian peacekeepers in the correct belief that the Belgium government would react by withdrawing its forces. Providing timely medical evacuation and emergency care is essential if third party forces are expected to put their lives on the line to protect innocents.

Depending on contractors to provide MEDEVAC services can be risky. When the situation deteriorated in Rwanda in 1994, for example, the two helicopters that the United Nations had contracted to provide this service simply disappeared. Lieutenant General Dallaire later commented, "with the country exploding, the pilots had fled to Uganda. They were both contract employees, so who could blame them? But the result was that we were confined to Kigali with no ability to evacuate casualties. In all likelihood any seriously wounded would die. In every decision I was to take over the coming weeks, I had to balance the risk of the operation against the fact that we had no medical safety net."[11]

The US military leads the world in the field of medical evacuation and emergency care: in Iraq, some 90 percent of wounded US soldiers survive, compared to some 75 percent during the Vietnam and Korean Wars and around 70 percent during World War II.[12] The Air Force's aeromedical evacuation teams and the large Air Force theater hospital at Balad, Iraq, have played an important role in saving US lives. Over 96 percent of injured service personnel who make it to the Balad field hospital survive, with urgent/priority patients air-evacuated within an average of 13.2 hours to even more capable facilities in Landstuhl, Germany, or the continental United States.[13] The Department of Defense's medical establishment is hard-pressed dealing with US casualties flowing in from Iraq and Afghanistan, but should a smaller American footprint in the Middle East result in decreased US casualties, the United States is capable of providing a critical niche service that regional and international peace-enforcement missions lack. The United States could boost the effectiveness of these efforts by offering mobile battalion aid stations, a small field hospital, and aeromedical-evacuation services. If appropriate, the United States could back intervention efforts by stationing hospital ships such as the USNS *Mercy* or USNS *Comfort* in the region to receive injured peace makers. These assets should not be seen as substitutes or alternatives to the large-scale efforts of NGOs such as the Red Cross, Doctors without Borders, and Refugees International, but rather as enabling components supporting the intervention forces that would create an environment where large-scale humanitarian intervention is possible.

CONCLUSION

Radio Suppression, Broadcasting Capability, and Strategic Communications Support

The case studies on Rwanda and the Côte d'Ivoire point out the importance of radio in instigating and organizing genocide (Radio RTLM in Rwanda) and in preventing it and garnering support for peace enforcement (ONUCI FM in Côte d'Ivoire). Over the course of the Cold War, the United States spent hundreds of millions of dollars on electronic warfare and has various platforms at its disposal, capable of conducting offensive electronic countermeasures such as jamming. In addition, the United States has devoted considerable thought and treasure to psychological operations and strategic communications. Currently, the US military has organizations and platforms capable of both message suppression and promulgation. The US Army's 4th Psychological Operations Group and the US Air Force's 193d Special Operations Wing have specialists trained in generating positive messages in support of operations, with the EC-130 Commando Solo aircraft capable of suppressing undesired radio broadcasts and substituting alternative radio transmission. These assets might not be deployed directly as part of an AETF supporting peace-enforcement and genocide-intervention operations, but the American commander should be aware of their potential and offer these capabilities to the mission commander if appropriate.

Coercive Airpower

As a final option, the United States can provide coercive capabilities to the peace-enforcement commander. The US Air Force has embraced this mission above all others, as evidenced by the pattern that every single chief of staff of the Air Force since its creation in 1947 has been either a bomber or fighter pilot. The US Air Force could certainly provide a wide array of coercive options to peace-enforcement commanders, but should remain reticent about employing coercive airpower for three reasons.

First, the intent of offering an airpower support package for peace enforcement is to assist and support the efforts of non-US led regional and international intervention missions. US forces should act as force multipliers for others and refrain from taking over and leading intervention efforts directly. Yet inevitably, once US coercive airpower is employed, our superior technology and capability will shift leadership of the intervention effort from other nations to ourselves. This might be justified if coercive airpower had a proven record of effectiveness in protecting civilians and stopping mass killings. This is far from the case. Airpower did indeed deter Saddam Hussein from crushing the Kurdish North of Iraq as he had the Shia South following his defeat in 1990, but it proved entirely ineffective in stopping Serb paramilitaries from driving out hundreds of thousands of Kosovars in 1999. Coercive airpower can act as a shield and sword for ground commanders, protecting ground forces and punishing those who attack them. It is far less effective at shielding civilians from light ground forces intent on slaughtering them, nor is it easy to distinguish perpetrators from victims from thousands of feet in the air.

This is a second reason to be wary of using coercive airpower for peace enforcement: the vaunted pinpoint accuracy of our weapon systems does not eliminate the possibility of civilian casualties and collateral damage. As Steffens points out in his case study on Somalia, the air strike against an alleged Somali National Alliance command center killed "up to 70 traditional clan leaders and civilians, most of them unassociated with Aideed." The use of coercive airpower may well have accomplished the opposite of its intended effect, increasing Aideed's influence and prestige rather than diminishing it. As for the feasibility of demolishing the killing barricades where Hutu militias massacred Tutsi civilians, this could hardly have been done without killing many of the civilian onlookers and cheerleaders. One might make the case that humanitarian war is justified, but the United States could well find itself scapegoated and pilloried, should it cause collateral damage in employing coercive airpower. We should set a high threshold before employing coercive airpower as an instrument of peace making: only after intervention ground forces have confronted, cajoled, and done their very best to stop mass killings from up close should we resort to doing so from far high in the skies.

Lastly, we should be wary of employing coercive airpower because of the cascading dynamics it will introduce into the

CONCLUSION

AETF or joint task force supporting genocide intervention efforts. Air mobility, communication support, aeromedical evacuation, and psychological operations will receive a smaller proportion of the commander's attention once he or she begins to tackle the challenge of employing coercive airpower. Nonetheless, should the intervention force commander need coercive airpower, some form of it should be available. The form and level of force will depend greatly on context. If intervening against groups that have no airpower or an extremely limited air force, then helicopter gunships, AV-8 Harrier aircraft, and AC-130 gunships will suffice. In cases where the enemy has an air force that needs to be deterred from operating, more advanced aircraft may be necessary. An element of coercive airpower should be put at the disposal of the intervening force in recognition of the wisdom of Pres. Theodore Roosevelt's adage "Speak softly and carry a big stick." Yet both the force commander and the AETF commander should think hard before employing that stick.

A wide array of actors is pressing for action to stop the mass slaughter of civilians. Yet genocide, while distinct from war in that it intentionally targets civilians and nonbelligerents for death, often occurs during warfare. Governments use the veil of war to exterminate entire groups they dislike or fear, simultaneously manipulating public wartime passions while stamping out dissent. Yet war is not genocide, nor is genocide war except in the sick rhetoric of its perpetrators. A growing consensus of domestic and international opinion is appalled when counterinsurgency campaigns veer toward the mass killing of entire populations, or when governments use foreign wars to root out and exterminate domestic opponents. As for the blatant slaughter of entire groups during peacetime, international opinion simply cannot accept that governments have the right to liquidate entire groups based on nothing more than their race, ethnicity, or religious affiliation.

The Convention on the Prevention and Punishment of the Crime of Genocide served as a first step in confronting the "crime that knows no name."[14] The convention, along with the work of scholars, survivors, and institutes devoted to understanding the Holocaust, sought to ensure that "never again" would be more than rhetoric. Yet as genocide after genocide unfolded since 1945 with little effective reaction, a growing number of people realized that one needed more than treaties, proclamations, and laws condemning genocide. One needed action. Cambodia, Rwanda, and the Balkans served as wake-up calls. Since then, a host of organizations and individuals has taken it upon themselves to spur the public conscience. Within the last 10 years, politicians from both the Democratic and Republican parties have spoken out against genocide. The secretary general of the United Nations has written an Action Plan to Prevent Genocide, and the president of the United States has included the topic of genocide prevention in the *National Security Strategy of the United States*. Despite this, operational concepts for stopping mass killings have been in short supply. This volume seeks to address the deficit by examining historical examples of genocide and genocide prevention. The case studies ask what was done and what might have been done, with Steffens, Stanley, Reeves, and Boyer offering both historical overviews and suggestions for the future. This volume focuses on one narrow component to genocide prevention and intervention: the use of airpower in stopping mass killings. If it in any way contributes to framing operational responses to the outbreak of genocide, the authors will have accomplished their purpose.

Notes

1. Feil, *Preventing Genocide*, 3.
2. Davis, *Anatomy of a Reform*.
3. Scott Feil's report differentiates between a safe haven and "safe sites." The former is appropriate where the targeted population is concentrated in one geographic area, such as the Kurds in Kurdistan. In Rwanda, where Hutus and Tutsis lived intermingled among each other, one would instead have had to create numerous local safe sites to protect the Tutsi.
4. Winn, "Air Force Propping up Peacekeepers in Darfur."
5. Office for the Coordination of Humanitarian Affairs, "Sudan."
6. Cooper and Mladenov, "Cote d'Ivoire, since 2002." Cooper notes that "US forces became involved as well. The USMC deployed C-130 Hercules transports, Sikorsky CH-53E Sea Stallion and UH-60L Blackhawk helicopters crewed by special forces to evacuate foreign nationals from Korhogo."
7. Dallaire and Beardsley, *Shake Hands with the Devil*, 203.
8. Ibid., 308.
9. Rohde, *Endgame*, 79.

CONCLUSION

10. British Broadcasting Corporation, "Africa's Troubled Darfur Mission."
11. Dallaire and Beardsley, *Shake Hands with the Devil*, 264.
12. Hyer, "Iraq and Afghanistan Producing New Pattern of Extremity War Injuries."
13. Ibid., and Seals, "Aeromedical Evacuation Teams Ready to Help Anytime."
14. Power, *A Problem from Hell*, chapter 2.

Contributors

Lt Col Aaron Steffens, USAF, is chief of International Developmental Fighter Programs for the deputy under secretary of the Air Force, International Affairs, in Washington, DC. He graduated from the US Air Force Academy in 1992 with a bachelor of science in aeronautical engineering degree and also holds a master of military operational art and science degree from the Air Command and Staff College, Maxwell AFB, Alabama, and a master of science degree from the College for Financial Planning, Phoenix, Arizona. He is a career fighter pilot with over 2,000 hours in the mighty F-16, including more than 200 combat missions over Iraq, the former Yugoslavia, and Afghanistan.

Lt Col Keith Reeves, USAF, is a 15-year Air Force veteran from Indianapolis, Indiana. He graduated from the United States Air Force Academy in 1992 and holds a master of engineering degree from the University of Colorado. Colonel Reeves started his career as a developmental engineer at Wright-Patterson AFB, Ohio, prior to entering pilot training. He then flew B-52s from Barksdale AFB, Louisiana, and held many positions including instructor pilot and wing combat plans officer. Colonel Reeves then transitioned to the B-2 at Whiteman AFB, Missouri, flew combat during Operation Iraqi Freedom, and instructed at the B-2 Formal Training Unit. In 2005 he attended the Air Command and Staff College. He is a senior pilot with more than 2,500 hours. He is currently chief of Air and Ground Dominance at Air Combat Command Headquarters, Langley AFB, Virginia.

CDR Timothy E. Boyer, USN, is a 1991 graduate of Purdue University with a bachelor of science degree in civil engineering. A naval flight officer, he has accumulated more than 2,700 hours in the E-2C Hawkeye. He has served operational tours with several east coast carrier airborne early warning squadrons, deploying to the Mediterranean and Arabian Gulf areas of operation on USS *America* (CV-66), USS *John F. Kennedy* (CV-67), and USS *George Washington* (CVN-73). He attended Air Command and Staff College and received a master of military operational art and science degree. He is currently serving as an information operations planner and chief of the US Central Command support division at the Joint Information Operations Warfare Command at Lackland AFB, Texas.

Maj George Stanley, USAF, is a native of Memphis, Tennessee, and graduated from the US Air Force Academy in 1994 with a bachelor of science degree in biochemistry. He attended undergraduate pilot training at Columbus AFB, Mississippi, and A-10 initial qualification training at Davis-Monthan AFB, Arizona. He has flown the A-10 from Pope AFB, North Carolina; Osan AB, Republic of Korea; and the A-10 Formal Training Unit at Davis-Monthan AFB; with two deployments in support of Operation Southern Watch. He attended Air Command and Staff College in 2005 and graduated with a master of arts in military operational art and science degree. He is a senior pilot with over 1,700 hours and is currently serving as the A-10 functional area manager at Air Combat Command, Langley AFB.

Bibliography

Allard, Kenneth. *Somalia Operations: Lessons Learned.* Washington, DC: National Defense University Press, 1995.

Annan, Kofi. "Action Plan to Prevent Genocide." *Preventgenocide.org.* http://www.preventgenocide.org/prevent/UNdocs/KofiAnnansActionPlantoPreventGenocide7Apr2004.htm.

Barnett, Michael. *Eyewitness to a Genocide: The United Nations and Rwanda.* Ithaca, NY: Cornell University Press, 2002.

Bax, Pauline. "Too Little, Too Late? UN Sanctions in Ivory Coast." *Radio Netherlands,* 8 February 2006. http://www.radionetherlands.nl/currentaffairs/ivo060208 (accessed 10 February 2006).

Bergen, Doris L. *War and Genocide: A Concise History of the Holocaust.* New York: Rowan and Littlefield Publishers, Inc., 2003.

Berman, Eric G., and Katie E. Sams. *Peacekeeping in Africa: Capabilities and Culpabilities.* Geneva: United Nations Publication, 2000.

Betts, Richard K. "The Delusion of Impartial Intervention." In *Turbulent Peace: The Challenges of Managing International Conflict.* Edited by Chester A. Crocker, Fen Osler Hampson, and Pamela Aall. Washington, DC: US Institute of Peace Press, 2001.

———. "The Delusion of Impartial Intervention." *Foreign Affairs* 73, no. 6 (November/December 1994): 20–33.

Blass, Thomas. "The Man Who Shocked the World: Thomas Blass Probes into the Life of Stanley Milgram, the Man Who Uncovered Some Disturbing Truths about Human Nature." *Psychology Today: Here to Help,* March/April 2002. http://www.psychologytoday.com/articles/pto-20020301-000037.html (accessed 5 February 2006).

British Broadcasting Corporation. "Africa's Troubled Darfur Mission," *BBC News,* 15 November 2007. http://news.bbc.co.uk/2/hi/africa/7097438.stm (accessed 17 January 2008).

———. "Country Profile: Ivory Coast." *BBC News.* http://news.bbc.co.uk/1/hi/world/Africa/country_profiles/1043014.stm (accessed 1 February 2006).

Brune, Lester H. *The United States and Post–Cold War Interventions: Bush and Clinton in Somalia, Haiti, and Bosnia, 1992–1998.* Claremont, CA: Regina Books, 1998.

Bureau of African Affairs, US Department of State. "Background Note: Cote d'Ivoire," January 2006. http://www.state.gov/r/pa/ei/bgn/2846.htm (accessed 1 February 2006).

Carafano, James Jay, and Nile Gardiner. "U.S. Military Assistance for Africa: A Better Solution." *Heritage Foundation*, October 2003. http://www.heritage.org/Research/Africa/bg1697.cfm (accessed 4 February 2006).

Carr, Caleb. "The Consequences of Somalia." *World Policy Journal* 10, no. 3 (Fall 1993): 1–5.

Carr Center for Human Rights Policy, John F. Kennedy School of Government, Harvard University. "National Security and Human Rights Program." *KSG.Harvard.edu.* http://www.ksg.harvard.edu/cchrp/programareas/nshr.php.

Carr, Lt Col Damian P. "Military Intervention during the Clinton Administration: A Critical Comparison." Strategy Research Project. Carlisle Barracks, PA: US Army War College, 2003.

Cassanelli, Lee V. "Somali Land Resource Issues in Historical Perspective." In *Learning from Somalia: The Lessons of Armed Humanitarian Intervention.* Edited by Walter Clarke and Jeffrey Herbst. Boulder, CO: Westview Press, 1997.

Cassel, Douglas W., Jr. "Genocide Warnings Should be Heeded." *Chicago Daily Law Bulletin* 1 (February 2006): 6.

Chirot, Daniel. "Chaos in Ivory Coast: Roots and Consequences." *Globalist,* 17 November 2004. http://www.theglobalist.com/DBWeb/StoryID.aspx?StoryID=4264 (accessed 24 January 2006).

Cilliers, Jakkie, and Mark Malan. "Progress with the African Standby Force." Institute for Security Studies Paper 98, May 2005. http://www.iss.co.za/pubs/papers/98/Paper98.htm.

Clarke, Walter. "Failed Visions and Uncertain Mandates in Somalia." In *Learning from Somalia: The Lessons of Armed Humanitarian Intervention.* Edited by Walter Clarke and Jeffrey Herbst. Boulder, CO: Westview Press, 1997.

Clarke, Walter, and Jeffrey Herbst. "Somalia and the Future of Humanitarian Intervention." In *Learning from Somalia: The Lessons of Armed Humanitarian Intervention.* Edited by

Walter Clarke and Jeffrey Herbst. Boulder, CO: Westview Press, 1997.

Clausewitz, Carl von. *On War*, ed. and trans. Michael Howard and Peter Paret. Princton, NJ: Princeton University Press, 1976.

Committee on Conscience, US Holocaust Memorial Museum. "Darfur Congressional Update." *Vital Voices on Genocide Prevention.* 24 November 2005. http://www.ushmm.org/conscience/analysis/details.php?content=2005-11-24.

———. "Genocide Prevention Task Force." *Responding to Threats of Genocide Today.* http://www.ushmm.org/conscience/taskforce/press/?content=2007-11-13.

———. *Responding to Threats of Genocide Today.* http://www.ushmm.org/conscience/.

"Conflict Country Briefings: Cote d'Ivoire, October 2005." *European Defense.* http://www.european-defence.co.uk/conflict briefings/ivorycoast.html (accessed 21 February 2006).

Cooper, Tom, and Alexander Mladenov. "Cote d'Ivoire, since 2002." *Air Combat Information Group*, 5 August 2004. http://www.acig.org/artman/publish/article_463.shtml (accessed 21 January 2008).

"Cost and Steps for Establishing and Operationalising the African Standby Force." *Institute for Security Studies*, October 2004. http://www.iss.co.za/AF/RegOrg/unity_to_union/pdfs/au/asf/costoct04.pdf (accessed 6 March 2006).

"Cote d'Ivoire: Country Report." East Syracuse, NY: Political Risk Services Group, 2006. http://www.prsonline.com/Report.aspx?country=Cote+d'Ivoire&file=players (accessed 9 February 2006).

"Crisis in Cote d'Ivoire." *Genocide Watch*, 11 December 2002. http://www.genocidewatch.org/CotedIvoireGenocide Watch.htm.

Crocker, Chester A. "The Lessons of Somalia." *Foreign Affairs* 74, no. 3 (May/June 1995): 2–8.

Dallaire, Lt Gen Roméo, and Brent Beardsley. *Shake Hands with the Devil: The Failure of Humanity in Rwanda.* Toronto: Random House Canada, 2003.

Davis, Richard G. *Anatomy of a Reform: The Expeditionary Aerospace Force.* Washington, DC: Air Force History and Museum Program, 2003.

de Coning, Cedric. "Refining the African Standby Force Concept." *Accord*, no. 2 (2004): 20–26.

Denning, Lt Col Mike. "Creating an Effective African Standby Force." *Parameters*, Winter 2004–2005. http://www.army.mil/professionalwriting/volumes/volume3/january_2005/1_05_1.html (accessed 2 March 2006).

Des Forges, Alison. *Leave No One to Tell the Story*. New York: Human Rights Watch, 1999.

Destexhe, Alain. *Rwanda and Genocide in the Twentieth Century*. Washington Square, NY: New York University Press, 1995.

di Giovanni, Janine. "Terror and Ethnic Cleansing in Ivory Coast." *Crimes of War Project*, 2 December 2002. http://www.crimesofwar.org/onnews/news-ivory.html.

Drysdale, John. "Foreign Military Intervention in Somalia." In *Learning from Somalia: The Lessons of Armed Humanitarian Intervention*, edited by Walter Clarke and Jeffrey Herbst. Boulder, CO: Westview Press, 1997.

Echevarria, Lt Col Antulio J., II, PhD. *An American Way of War or Way of Battle*. Carlisle, PA: Stategic Studies Institute, US Army War College, 2004. http://www.strategicstudiesinstitute.army.mil/pdffiles/PUB374.pdf.

"ECOWAS [Economic Community of West African States] 'Rapid Reaction Force.'" *Africa Research Bulletin: Political, Social and Cultural Series* 41, no. 6 (July 2004): 15822.

"Fact Sheet: Iraqi War." *InfoPlease Almanacs*, 31 March 2004. http://www.infoplease.com/ipa/A0908900.html (accessed 6 March 2006).

Feil, Scott R., Col, USA. "A Rwandan Retrospective: Developing an Intervention Option, a Report to the Carnegie Commission on Preventing Deadly Conflict." Carlisle Barracks, PA: US Army War College, 1997.

———. *Preventing Genocide: How the Early Use of Force Might Have Succeeded in Rwanda*. A Report to the Carnegie Commission on Preventing Deadly Conflict. New York: Carnegie Corporation, 1998.

Gberie, Lansana, and Prosper Addo. *Challenges of Peace Implementation in Cote d'Ivoire: Report on an Expert Workshop by KAIPTC and ZIF* [Kofi Annan International Peacekeeping Training Center and *Zentrum für Internationale Friedenseinsätze* (Center for International Peace Operations)]. Institute for Security Studies, Monograph No. 105, August 2004. http://www.issafrica.org/pubs/Monographs/No105/Contents.html.

Genocide Intervention Network. "Darfur Legislation." *DarfurScores.org, Calling on Congress to Stop Genocide.* http://www.darfurscores.org/darfur-legislation.

Genocide Prevention Task Force, US Holocaust Memorial Museum. 13 November 2007. http://www.ushmm.org/conscience/taskforce/press/?content=2007-11-13.

Genocide Studies Program, Yale University. http://www.yale.edu/gsp/.

"Genocide Watch Has Three Levels of Genocide Alerts®." *Genocide Watch.* http://www.genocidewatch.org/alerts/alerts.htm (accessed 15 November 2007).

Ghormley, Maj Gen T. F. "Command Philosophy." United States Central Command, Combined Joint Task Force—Horn of Africa, undated. http://www.hoa.centcom.mil/Philosophy.pdf (accessed 23 February 2006).

Goldstone, Jack A., et al. *State Failure Task Force Report: Phase III Findings.* McLean, VA: Science Applications International Corporation (SAIC), 2000. http://www.cidcm.umd.edu/publications/papers/SFTF%20Phase%20III%20Report%20Final.pdf.

Gourevitch, Philip. *We Wish to Inform You that Tomorrow We Will Be Killed with Our Families: Stories from Rwanda.* New York: Farrar, Straus, and Giroux, 1998.

Gregston, Brent. "Rwanda Syndrome on the Ivory Coast." *Worldpress.org,* 30 November 2004. http://www.worldpress.org/Africa/1986.cfm (accessed 24 January 2006).

Harff, Barbara. "Assessing Risks of Genocide and Politicide." In *Peace and Conflict 2005: A Global Survey of Armed Conflicts, Self-Determination Movements, and Democracy.* Edited by Monty G. Marshall, Ted Robert Gurr, and University of Maryland (College Park MD). Center for International Development and Conflict Management. College Park, MD: Center for International Development and Conflict Management, 2005, 57–61.

———. "No Lessons Learned from the Holocaust? Assessing Risks of Genocide and Political Mass Murder since 1955."

American Political Science Review 97, no. 1 (February 2003): 57–73.

Hatzfeld, Jean. *Machete Season: The Killers in Rwanda Speak.* New York: Farrar, Straus, and Giroux, 2005.

Henderson, Errol Anthony. *Democracy and War: The End of an Illusion?* Boulder, CO: Lynne Rienner Publishers, 2002.

Henk, Dan, and Steven Metz. *The United States and the Transformation of African Security: The African Crisis Response Initiative and Beyond.* Carlisle, PA: Strategic Studies Institute, US Army War College, December 1997.

Henry L. Stimson Center. "Research Programs: Future of Peace Operations Program." *Stimson.org.* http://www.stimson.org/fopo/programhome.cfm.

Hewitt, William. *Defining the Horrific: Readings on Genocide and Holocaust in the 20th Century.* Upper Saddle River, NJ: Prentice Hall, 2004.

Hicks, Maj J. Marcus. "Fire in the City: Airpower in Urban, Smaller-Scale Contingencies." School of Advanced Airpower Studies thesis, Air University, June 1999. https://research.maxwell.af.mil/papers/ay1999/saas/hicks-jm.pdf.

Hilberg, Raul. *The Destruction of the European Jews.* London: W. H. Allen, 1961.

———. *The Destruction of the European Jews.* New York: Holmes & Meier, 1985.

Hippel, Karin von. *Democracy by Force: US Military Intervention in the Post–Cold War World.* Cambridge: University Press, 2000.

Hirsch, John L., and Robert B. Oakley. *Somalia and Operation Restore Hope: Reflections on Peacemaking and Peacekeeping.* Washington, DC: United States Institute of Peace Press, 1995.

History and American Studies, University of Mary Washington. "The James Farmer Professor in Human Rights." http://www.umw.edu/cas/history/james_farmer_professorship/james_farmer_professor/default.php.

"Holocaust Scholar Raul Hilberg Dies at 81." *Associated Press,* 6 August 2007. http://www.iht.com/articles/ap/2007/08/06/america/NA-GEN-US-Obit-Hilberg.php.

Holt, Victoria, and Tobias Berkman. *The Impossible Mandate? Military Preparedness, The Responsibility to Protect and*

Modern Peace Operations. Washington, DC: Henry L. Stimson Center, 2006.

Howe, Jonathan T. "Relations between the United States and the UN in Somalia." In *Learning from Somalia: The Lessons of Armed Humanitarian Intervention*. Edited by Walter Clarke and Jeffrey Herbst. Boulder, CO: Westview Press, 1997.

Human Rights Watch. "Cote d'Ivoire." *Human Rights Overview*, January 2004. http://hrw.org/English/docs/2004/01/21/cotedi6973.htm (accessed 9 April 2006).

———. "Cote d'Ivoire: The Human Rights Cost of the Political Impasse." *Human Rights Watch Report*, 21 December 2005. http://hrw.org/backgrounder/africa/cote1205/.

Hutcheson, Keith. *Air Mobility: The Evolution of Global Reach*. Vienna, VA: Point One and VII Publishing, 1999.

Hyer, Richard. "Iraq and Afghanistan Producing New Pattern of Extremity War Injuries." *Medscape: Medical News*, 27 March 2006. http://www.medscape.com/viewarticle/528624.

"Information on the Genocide Convention." *PreventGenocide.org*. http://www.preventgenocide.org/law/convention/ .

"The International Campaign to End Genocide." *GenocideWatch.org*. http://www.genocidewatch.org/internationalcampaign.htm (accessed 10 February 2006).

International Crisis Group. "Conflict History: Côte d'Ivoire." *CrisisGroup.org*, 2006. http://www.crisisgroup.org/home/index.cfm?action=conflict_search&1=1&t=1&c_country.

———. "Côte d'Ivoire: Halfway Measures Will Not Suffice." *Africa Briefing* no. 33, 12 October 2005. http://www.crisisgroup.org/home/index.cfm?l=1&id=3746.

———. "Côte d'Ivoire: No Peace in Sight." *Africa Briefing* no. 82, 12 July 2004. http://www.crisisgroup.org/home/index.cfm?id=2858&1=1.

———. "Côte d'Ivoire: The War is Not Yet Over." *Africa Report* 72, 28 November 2003. http://www.crisisgroup.org/home/index.cfm?id=2389&1=1.

Itano, Nicole. "Next Door, Lessons for Liberia: Western Troops and African Peacekeepers Teamed Up to End the Ivory Coast Civil War." *Christian Science Monitor*, 30 July 2003.

Jane's SENTINEL Security Assessment: West Africa 9. Surrey, UK: Jane's Information Group Limited, 2005.

Joint Publication (JP) 3-0. *Doctrine for Joint Operations*, 10 September 2001.

JP 3-0. *Doctrine for Joint Operations: Revision Final Coordination*, 23 December 2005.

JP 3-07. *Joint Doctrine for Military Operations Other Than War*, 16 June 1995.

JP 3-07.3. *Peace Operations*, 17 October 2007.

JP 3-07.6. *Joint Tactics, Techniques, and Procedures for Foreign Humanitarian Assistance*, 15 August 2001.

JP 3-57. *Joint Doctrine for Civil-Military Operations*, 8 February 2001.

Kamukama, Dixon. *Rwanda Conflict*. Kampala, Uganda: Fountain Publishers, 1997.

Kennedy, Kevin M. "The Military and Humanitarian Organizations." In *Learning from Somalia: The Lessons of Armed Humanitarian Intervention*. Edited by Walter Clarke and Jeffrey Herbst. Boulder, CO: Westview Press, 1997.

Kent, Vanessa, and Mark Malan. "The African Standby Force: Progress and Prospects." *African Security Review* 12, no. 3 (2003): 71–81.

Khan, Shaharyar M. *The Shallow Graves of Rwanda*. New York: I. B. Tauris Publishers, 2000.

Kiernan, Ben. *Blood and Soil: A World History of Genocide and Extermination from Sparta to Darfur*. New Haven, CT: Yale University Press, 2007.

———. "The Cambodian Genocide 1975–1979." In *Century of Genocide: Critical Essays and Eyewitness Accounts*. Edited by Samuel Totten, William S. Parsons, and Israel W. Charny, 339–73. New York: Routledge, 2004.

Kilcullen, Lt Col David, PhD., Royal Australian Army. "Counter Global Insurgency: A Strategy for the War on Terrorism." *US Marine Corps Small Wars Center of Excellence*. http://www.smallwars.quantico.usmc.mil/search/Articles/CounteringGlobalInsurgency.pdf (accessed 16 January 2006).

Kuperman, Alan J. *The Limits of Humanitarian Intervention: Genocide in Rwanda*. Washington, DC: Brookings Institution Press, 2001.

Lattimer, Mark. "Peoples under Threat." *State of the World's Minorities 2006*. London: Minority Rights Group International 2005, 8–16. http://www.minorityrights.org/download.php?id=18.

Lemkin, Raphael. *Axis Rule in Occupied Europe: Laws of Occupation—Analysis of Government—Proposals for Redress.* Washington, DC: Carnegie Endowment for International Peace, 1944.

Lewis, I. M. *A Modern History of Somalia.* Boulder, CO: Westview Press, 1988.

Makinda, Samuel M. *Seeking Peace from Chaos: Humanitarian Intervention in Somalia.* Boulder, CO: Lynne Rienner Publishers, Inc., 1993.

Martin, Douglas. "Raul Hilberg, 81, Historian Who Wrote of the Holocaust as a Bureaucracy, Dies." *New York Times*, 7 August 2007. http://www.nytimes.com/2007/08/07/us/07hilberg.html?_r=1&oref=slogin.

McMahon, Robert. "UN: Powell Calls Darfur Atrocities 'Genocide,' as Debate Begins on New Resolution." *Radio Free Europe*, 2004. http://www.rferl.org/featuresarticle/2004/9/CDB82A4B-4BEB-43B1-819B-A914BE5F8856.html.

Melvern, Linda. *Conspiracy to Murder: The Rwandan Genocide.* London and New York: Verso, 2004.

Menkhaus, Ken, and Louis Ortmayer. *Key Decisions in the Somalia Intervention.* Washington, DC: Institute for the Study of Diplomacy, Georgetown University, 1995.

Merrill, Austin. "Citizen Soldiers." *New Republic* 233, no. 16, (17 October 2005): 14.

"Military: Operation Provide Relief." *GlobalSecurity.org*, 27 May 2004. http://www.globalsecurity.org/military/ops/provide_relief.htm (accessed 10 February 2006).

Mills, Nicholas, and Kira Brunner, eds. *The New Killing Fields.* New York: Basic Books, 2002.

Mironko, Charles K. "Iberito: Means and Motive in the Rwandan Genocide." *Yale Center for International and Area Studies Working Papers Database.* http://research.yale.edu/ycias/database/files/GS23.pdf.

Montreal Institute for Genocide and Human Rights Studies. http://migs.concordia.ca/.

Ofcansky, Thomas. "Chapter 5–National Security: Human Rights." In *Somalia: A Country Study.* Edited by Helen Chapin Metz. Washington, DC: Federal Research Division,

Library of Congress, 1993. http://lcweb2.loc.gov/frd/cs/sotoc.html (accessed 21 December 2005).

Office for the Coordination of Humanitarian Affairs, United Nations. "IRIN [Integrated Regional Information Networks] Webspecial: A Decent Burial." *IRINNews.org*, 2001. http://www.irinnews.org/webspecials/somaliajustice/interviewsnm.asp (accessed 23 December 2005).

———. "Sudan: Waiting for Peacekeeping Muscle in Darfur," *IRINNews.org*, 22 January 2008. http://www.irinnews.org/Report.aspx?ReportId=76050 (accessed 22 January 2008).

Office of the Deputy Assistant Secretary of Defense for Middle East/Africa Region, Department of Defense. Discussion Paper, 1 May 1994. http://www.gwu.edu/~nsarchiv/NSAEBB/NSAEBB53/rw050194.pdf.

Office of the High Commissioner for Human Rights, United Nations. "Convention on the Prevention and Punishment of the Crime of Genocide." http://www.unhchr.ch/html/menu3/b/p_genoci.htm.

"Operations and Initiatives." *US European Command*, January 2006. http://www.eucom.mil/english/Operations/main.asp (accessed 6 March 2006).

Orentlicher, Diane F. "Genocide." In *Defining the Horrific: Readings on Genocide and Holocaust in the Twentieth Century*. Edited by William L. Hewitt. Upper Saddle River, NJ: Pearson, 2004.

Paret, Peter, ed. *Makers of Modern Strategy from Machiavelli to the Nuclear Age.* Princeton, NJ: Princeton University Press, 1986.

Peace and Security Section, United Nations Department of Public Information. "The United Nations and Darfur, Fact Sheet." http://www.un.org/News/dh/infocus/sudan/fact_sheet.pdf.

Power, Samantha. *A Problem from Hell: America and the Age of Genocide.* New York: Basic Books, 2002.

———. "Bystanders to Genocide." *Atlantic Monthly*, September 2001. http://www.theatlantic.com/doc/200109/power-genocide (accessed 9 April 2006).

Press Release. "Somali Community of the Americas," 18 March 1991. http://www.somaliawatch.org/archivefeb01/010202301.htm (accessed 21 December 2005).

Prunier, Gérard. *The Rwanda Crisis: History of a Genocide.* New York: Columbia University Press, 1995.

Purvis, Andrew. "One Lesson worth Remembering." *Time Europe* 158, no. 21 (November 2001): 45–46.

Refugees International. http://www.refugeesinternational.org/.

Rohde, David. *Endgame: The Betrayal and Fall of Srebrenica, Europe's Worst Massacre since World War II.* 1st ed. New York: Farrar, Straus, and Giroux, 1997.

Rotberg, Robert I. "The Lessons of Somalia for U.S. Foreign Policy." In *Learning from Somalia: The Lessons of Armed Humanitarian Intervention.* Edited by Walter Clarke and Jeffrey Herbst. Boulder, CO: Westview Press, 1997.

Rummel, R. J. *Death by Government.* New Brunswick, NJ: Transactions Publishers, 1994.

———. *Never Again: Ending War, Democide, and Famine through Democratic Freedom.* Coral Springs, FL: Llumina Press, 2005.

———. *Statistics of Democide: Genocide and Mass Murder since 1900.* Charlottesville, VA: Center for National Security Law, 1995.

"Rwanda: Population." *Institute for Security Studies*, February 2005. http://www.issafrica.org/AF/profiles/Rwanda/Population.html (accessed 1 Mar 2006).

Sahnoun, Mohamed. *Somalia: The Missed Opportunities.* Washington, DC: United States Institute of Peace Press, 1994.

Salih, M. A. Mohamed, and Lennart Wohlgemuth, eds. *Crisis Management and the Politics of Reconciliation in Somalia: Statements from the Uppsala Forum, 17–19 January 1994.* Sweden: Reprocentralen HSC, 1994.

Samatar, Said S. "Chapter 1–The Historical Setting: Somalia's Difficult Decade, 1980–1990, Harrying the Hawiye." In *Somalia: A Country Study.* Edited by Helen Chapin Metz. Washington, DC: Federal Research Division, Library of Congress, 1993. http://lcweb2.loc.gov/frd/cs/sotoc.html (accessed 21 December 2005).

———."Chapter 1–The Historical Setting: Somalia's Difficult Decade, 1980–1990, Oppression of the Isaaq." In *Somalia: A Country Study.* Edited by Helen Chapin Metz. Washington, DC: Federal Research Division, Library of Congress, 1993. http://lcweb2.loc.gov/frd/cs/sotoc.html (accessed 21 December 2005).

———. "Chapter 1–The Historical Setting: Somalia's Difficult Decade, 1980–1990, Persecution of the Majerteen." In *Somalia: A Country Study*. Edited by Helen Chapin Metz. Washington, DC: Federal Research Division, Library of Congress, 1993. http://lcweb2.loc.gov/frd/cs/sotoc.html (accessed 21 December 2005).

Save Darfur Coalition. "September Briefing Paper: The Genocide in Darfur." *SaveDarfur.org*. http://www.savedarfur.org/newsroom/policypapers/september_briefing_paper_the_genocide_in_darfur/.

Scherrer, Christian P. *Genocide and Crisis in Central Africa: Conflict Roots, Mass Violence, and Regional War*. Westport, CT: Praeger Publishers, 2002.

Schlein, Lisa. "UN Expert Says Action Needed to Prevent Genocide in Several African Countries." *Voice of America, Geneva*, 27 January 2006. http://www.voanews.com/english/2006-01-27-voa58.cfm.

Seals, Craig. "Aeromedical Evacuation Teams Ready to Help Anytime." *Air Force News*, 25 June 2007. http://www.af.mil/news/story.asp?id=123058500 (accessed 25 January 2008).

Sommer, John G. *Hope Restored? Humanitarian Aid in Somalia 1990–1994*. Refugee Policy Group Report. Washington, DC: Center for Policy Analysis and Research on Refugee Issues, November 1994.

"Somalia Beyond the Warlords: The Need for a Verdict on Human Rights Abuses." *Human Rights Watch Publications* 5, no. 2 (7 March 1993). http://www.hrw.org/reports/1993/somalia (accessed 21 December 2005).

Stanton, Gregory H. "Genocides, Politicides, and Other Mass Murder since 1945, With Stages in 2005." *Genocide Watch*, 2005. http://www.genocidewatch.org/genocidetable2005.htm (accessed 10 January 2006).

———. "The Eight Stages of Genocide." *Genocide Watch*, 1996. http://www.genocidewatch.org/8stages1996.htm.

———. "The Eight Stages of Genocide." *Genocide Watch*, 1998. http://www.genocidewatch.org/8stages.htm.

"Statement of the Honorable Walter H. Kansteiner III, Assistant Secretary, Bureau of African Affairs, US Department of State." In *Prospects for Peace in Ivory Coast: Hearing before the Subcommittee on Africa of the Committee on International Relations.* 108th Cong., 1st sess., 12 February 2003, 11.

"Statement of Timothy Docking, Ph.D., Program Officer, Research and Studies Program, US Institute of Peace." In *Prospects for Peace in Ivory Coast: Hearing before the Subcommittee on Africa of the Committee on International Relations.* 108th Cong., 1st sess., 12 February 2003, 22.

Stridsberg, Peter. "Cote d'Ivoire Historical Background: A Study of the Risk for Genocide." *Dictator of the Month.* http://dictatorofthemonth.com/English/Articles/Ivory_Coast_genocide_risk.htm (accessed 21 November 2005).

Student Anti-Genocide Coalition. http://standnow.org/.

Thibodeaux, Raymond. "Ivory Coast Fears a Wider War." *Boston Globe,* 20 October 2002. http://proquest.umi.com/pqdweb?did=217151331&sid=2&Fmt=3&clientld=417&RQT=309&VName=PQD (accessed 9 February 2006).

Tomlinson, Chris. "US General Calls Somalia Terror Haven," *ABC News International,* 13 May 2005. http://abcnews.go.com/International/wireStory?id=755053 (accessed 23 February 2006).

Totten, Samuel, Paul R. Bartrop, and Steven L. Jacobs, eds. *Dictionary of Genocide.* Westport, CT: Greenwood Press, 2007.

Totten, Samuel, William S. Parsons, and Israel W. Charny, eds. *Century of Genocide: Critical Essays and Eyewitness Accounts.* 2nd ed. New York: Routledge, 2004.

Tubbs, James O. *Beyond Gunboat Diplomacy: Forceful Applications of Airpower in Peace Enforcement Operations.* Maxwell AFB, AL: Air University Press, 1997.

UN Security Council Resolution (UNSCR) 1572. United Nations Security Council, 5078th meeting, 15 November 2004. http://www.onuci.org/pdf_fr/pio/resolution1572_e.pdf.

UNSCR 1721. United Nations Security Council, 5561st meeting, 1 November 2006. http://daccessdds.un.org/doc/UNDOC/GEN/N06/597/36/PDF/N0659736.pdf?OpenElement.

United Nations. "Annan Chooses Former Political Prisoner as His First Special Advisor on Genocide." *UN News Centre,* 12 July 2004. http://www0.un.org/apps/news/story.asp?NewsID=11312&Cr=genocide&Cr1= (accessed 5 April 2006).

———. "Decision on Follow-up to the Declaration on the Prevention of Genocide: Indicators of Patterns of Systematic and Massive Racial Discrimination." *Committee on the Elimination of Racial Discrimination*, 67th session, 14 October 2005. http://www2.ohchr.org/english/bodies/cerd/docs/indicators_for_genocide.doc.

———. "Report of the Panel on United Nations Peace Operations." *UN.org.* http://www.un.org/peace/reports/peace_operations/.

United Nations Mission in Côte d'Ivoire. "Cote d'Ivoire-MINUCI [Mission des Nations Unies en Côte d'Ivoire]-Mandate." http://www.un.org/Depts/dpko/missions/minuci/mandate.html.

United Nations Operation in Côte d'Ivoire [UNOCI]. "Côte d'Ivoire-UNOCI-Mandate." http://www.un.org/Depts/dpko/missions/unoci/mandate.html.

———. "Facts and Figures." http://www.un.org/Depts/dpko/missions/unoci/facts.html (accessed 28 November 2006).

US Africa Command. "Questions and Answers about AFRICOM." http://www.africom.mil/africomFAQs.asp.

US Department of Defense. *National Defense Strategy of the United States of America.* Washington, DC: Department of Defense, March 2005.

US Department of State. "Press Statement." 19 September 2006. http://www.state.gov/r/pa/prs/ps/2006/72830.htm.

Valentino, Benjamin A. *Final Solutions: Mass Killing and Genocide in the Twentieth Century.* Ithaca, NY: Cornell University Press, 2004.

"Weinberger Doctrine." *Wikipedia.* 10 December 2005. http://en.wikipedia.org/wiki/Weinberger_doctrine (accessed 10 January 2006).

Weinberger, Hon. Caspar W., secretary of defense. "Remarks Prepared for Delivery to the National Press Club, Washington, DC, 28 November 1984." *PBS Online* and *WGBH/FRONTLINE*, 1999. http://www.pbs.org/wgbh/pages/frontline/shows/military/force/weinberger.html.

Weiss, Thomas G. "Rekindling Hope in UN Humanitarian Intervention." In *Learning from Somalia: The Lessons of Armed Humanitarian Intervention.* Edited by Walter Clarke and Jeffrey Herbst. Boulder, CO: Westview Press, 1997.

Weiss-Wendt, Anton. "Hostage of Politics: Raphael Lemkin On 'Soviet Genocide.' " *Journal of Genocide Research* 7, no. 4 (2005).

Weitz, Eric D. *A Century of Genocide: Utopias of Race and Nation.* Princeton, NJ: Princeton University Press, 2003.

The White House. *National Security Strategy of the United States of America.* Washington, DC: 2002. http://www.whitehouse.gov/nsc/nss/2002/index.html.

———. *National Security Strategy of the United States of America.* Washington, DC: 2006. http://www.whitehouse.gov/nsc/nss/2006/.

Winn, Patrick. "Air Force Propping up Peacekeepers in Darfur." *Air Force Times*, 30 October 2007. http://www.airforcetimes.com/news/2007/10/airforce_africa_darfur_071029w/ (accessed 21 January 2008).

Wisner, Frank G. Office of the Under Secretary of Defense. To Sandy Berger, deputy assistant to the president for National Security Affairs, National Security Council. Memorandum. "Subject: Rwanda—Jamming Civilian Radio Broadcasts." 5 May 1994. http://www.gwu.edu/~nsarchiv/NSAEBB/NSAEBB53/rw050594.pdf.

Woods, James L. "U.S. Government Decisionmaking Processes during Humanitarian Operations in Somalia." In *Learning from Somalia: The Lessons of Armed Humanitarian Intervention.* Edited by Walter Clarke and Jeffrey Herbst. Boulder, CO: Westview Press, 1997.

Yale University. "Genocide Studies Program Links." http://www.yale.edu/gsp/links/index.html.

Index

Acra III, 107
Action Plan to Prevent Genocide, 7, 18, 141
Addis Ababa, Ethiopia, 28, 40
Afghanistan, 21, 39, 44, 132, 136–37
Africa, 21–25, 35, 44, 46, 50–51, 54, 67, 71–72, 81, 96, 99–103, 118, 123
Africa Contingency Operations Training and Assistance Program, 46
Africa Watch, 23–25
African, 7, 22, 25–26, 43–47, 50–51, 61, 66, 72, 96, 101–2, 107, 112, 114–16, 122–25, 133, 135
African Standby Force, 44, 50–51. *See also* ASF
African Union, 7, 45, 96, 107, 133, 135. *See also* AU
AH-1, 34, 43. *See also* aircraft and helicopters
AH-6, 43. *See also* aircraft and helicopters
Aideed, Mohamed Farah, 23–24, 26–28, 32–34, 37, 43, 66, 139
Air Corps Tactical School, 130
Air Force Theater Hospital, Balad, Iraq, 137
Air Mobility Command, 29. *See also* AMC
aircraft, 27, 29, 42–43, 64, 69–71, 114, 123, 129–31, 134, 136, 138, 140. *See also* helicopters
   AH-1, 34, 43
   AH-6, 43
   AV-8 Harrier, 140
   C-17, 133
   C-130, 29, 141
   C-160, 114, 131
   CH-47, 134
   Commando Solo, 70, 129, 138 (*see also* EC-130)
   EC-130, 47, 70, 129, 138 (*see also* Commando Solo)
   Fennec (Puma) light helicopter, 134
   MH-60, 43
   MV-22 Osprey, 134
   RQ-1 Predator UAV, 47 (*see also* unmanned aerial vehicles and UAV)
   RQ-4 Global Hawk, 136 (*see also* unmanned aerial vehicles and UAV)
   SA.330 Cougar helicopters, 134
   Unmanned aerial vehicles, 136 (*see also* UAV)
Akazu, 62, 86–89, 91–92, 94, 96–97
Albright, Madeleine, 3
Algerian, 25
Alliance des Militaires Agacés par les Séculaires Actes Sournois des Unaristes, 88. *See also* Alliance of Soldiers Provoked by the Age-old Deceitful Acts of the Unarists and AMASASU
Alliance of Soldiers Provoked by the Age-old Deceitful Acts of the Unarists, 88. *See also Alliance des Militaires Agacés par les Séculaires Actes Sournois des Unaristes* and AMASASU
Alliot-Marie, Michele, 119
AMASASU, 86, 88–89. *See also Alliance des Militaires Agacés par les Séculaires Actes Sournois des Unaristes* and Alliance of Soldiers Provoked by the Age-old Deceitful Acts of the Unarists
AMC, 29, 42. *See also* Air Materiel Command
America, 2, 38, 44, 49, 80, 121
American, 2, 5–6, 16, 21–22, 28, 30–31, 34–38, 44, 46–47, 66–67, 72, 79–80, 96, 99, 137–38
American Academy of Diplomacy, 16
American Bar Association, 5
Amnesty International, 10, 25
Annan, Kofi, 7, 15, 18, 121, 125
anti-French, 107, 114–15. *See also* France and French
anti-Gbagbo, 107. *See also* Gbagbo, Laurent
anti-semitism, 4
anti-USC, 23. *See also* United Somali Congress
APROSOMA, 58–59. *See also Association Pour la Promotion Sociale de la Masse* and Association for the Social Promotion of the Masses
Armenia, 84
Armenian, 1
Arusha Accords, 62–63, 66, 71, 78, 86
ASF, 44–47. *See also* African Standby Force

INDEX

ASF-designed, 47. *See also* African Standby Force
Aspin, Les, 34
Association for the Social Promotion of the Masses, 58. *See also Association Pour la Promotion Sociale de la Masse* and APROSOMA
Association Pour la Promotion Sociale de la Masse, 58. *See also* Association for the Social Promotion of the Masses and APROSOMA
Assyrian, 4
AU, 7, 45–47, 91. *See also* African Union
AV-8, 140. *See also* aircraft

Bahutu Manifesto, 58–59
Balad, Iraq, 137
Ban Ki-moon, 4, 7, 105, 110, 133
Barnett, Michael, 77, 98–99
Barre, Said, 21–26
Battle of Mogadishu, Somalia, 21, 34–35, 38, 44
Bédié, Henri Konan, 104–5, 110
Belgian, 29, 55–60, 66, 68, 77, 136
Belgium, 57, 66, 68, 72, 136
Biden, Joseph, 3
Bir, Cevik, 33
Bosnia, 1, 6, 67, 132
Bosnian, 1, 6
Bouaké, Côte d'Ivoire, 114
Boutros-Ghali, Boutros, 27–28, 31–32
British, 9, 112, 124–25, 142
Brownback, Sam, 3, 17
Bujumbura, Burundi, 70–71
Burao, Somalia, 23
Burke, Edmund, 72
Burkina Faso, 102, 104
Burma, 1
Burundi, 59–64, 70–71
Bush, George H. W., 31
Bush, George W., 2, 31

C-17, 133. *See also* aircraft
C-130, 29, 141. *See also* aircraft
C-160, 114, 131. *See also* aircraft
Cambodia, 1, 84, 141
Cambodian, 2, 6, 12, 18, 85
Canadian, 15, 29
Capuano, Michael, 3
Carnegie Commission on Preventing Deadly Conflict, 68–69
Carr Center for Human Rights Policy, Harvard University, 16. *See also* Harvard University, Carr Center for Human Rights Policy
CDR, 62, 88, 101. *See also Coalition pour la Défense de la Republique* and Coalition for the Defense of the Republic
cease-fire, 26, 32, 61, 106–7, 114, 116–17
CENTCOM, 29–31, 35, 42. *See also* US Central Command
Center for International Development and Conflict Management's State Failure Task Force, 108
CERD, 109, 113, 131. *See also* Committee on the Elimination of Racial Discrimination and UN Committee on the Elimination of Racial Discrimination
CH-47, 134. *See also* aircraft and helicopters
Chad, 1
chapter VI, Charter of the United Nations, 15, 28, 45. *See also* UN Charter Chapter VI
chapter VII, Charter of the United Nations, 15, 31, 33, 39, 68, 116. *See also* UN Charter Chapter VII
Charleston AFB, SC, 133
Charter of the United Nations, 6, 7
Chinese, 6
5me Régiment d'Hélicoptères de Combat, Aviation Légère de L'Armée de Terre, 134. *See also* 5th French Army Aviation Combat Helicopter Regiment and 5 RHC
Civil Military Operations Center, 42. *See also* CMOC
civil war, 6, 21–22, 24–26, 39, 60, 65, 67–68, 70, 93, 102–3, 105, 107–8, 111, 113
civil-affairs, 31
civil-military, 46, 50
CJTF-HOA, 35–36. *See also* Combined Joint Task Force-Horn of Africa
clan, 22–25, 29, 34, 128, 139
Clarke, Walter, 48n–50n, 82
Clausewitz, Carl von, 82, 99
Clinton, Bill, 34
Clinton, Hillary, 3
CMOC, 42. *See also* Combined Military Operations Center
Coalition for the Defense of the Republic, 88. *See also Coalition pour la Défense de la Republique* and CDR

Coalition pour la Défense de la République, 88. *See also* Coalition for the Defense of the Republic and CDR
codeployed, 45
Cohen, 3
Cold War, 6–8, 26–27, 31, 48–50, 58, 67, 138
Combined Joint Task Force-Horn of Africa, 35. *See also* CJTF-HOA
Commandement des Opérations Spéciales, 134. *See also* French Special Operations Command and COS
Commando Solo, 70, 129, 138. *See also* EC-130 and aircraft
Committee on Conscience, 1, 10, 17
Committee on the Elimination of Racial Discrimination, 109. *See also* UN Committee on the Elimination of Racial Discrimination and CERD
Congo, 59, 77, 96, 132, 136
Congress, 23, 28, 34, 37, 81
Convention on the Prevention and Punishment of the Crime of Genocide, 4–5, 7, 18–19, 140
COS, 134. *See also Commandement des Opérations Spéciales* and French Special Operations Command
Côte d'Ivoire, 101–25, 128, 131, 134, 138
Côte d'Ivoire Student Federation, 112. *See also Fédération Estudiantine et Scolaire de Côte d'Ivoire* and FESCI
Cultural Revolution, 6
Cyangugu, Rwanda, 70

Dallaire, Roméo, 53, 66–69, 135, 137
Daloa, Côte d'Ivoire, 111
Darfur, 1–3, 6–7, 17–18, 128, 132–33, 135–36,
DDR, 107. *See also* demobilization, disarmament, and reintegration
demobilization, disarmament, and reintegration, 107. *See also* DDR
Democide, 8–9, 18–19
Democratic, 3, 9, 19, 58–59, 80, 101, 103, 113, 117–18,
Democratic Party of Côte d'Ivoire, 103. *See also Parti Democratique de la Côte d'Ivoire* and PDCI
Democratic Republic of Congo, 59
Democratic Republican Movement-Party of the Movement for Emancipation of the Hutu People, 58. *See also Mouvement Démocratique Républicain-Parti du Mouvement de l'Emancipation du Peuple Hutu* and MDR-PARMEHUTU
Department of State, 2, 7, 25. *See also* DOS
di Giovanni, Janine, 112
Diarra, Seydou, 106
Dioula (ethic group, Côte d'Ivoire), 111
Djibouti, 26
Doctors without Borders, 137
DOS, 25, 28. *See also* Department of State
Durbin, South Africa, 3

East Africa, 35
Eastern Europe, 4
EC-130, 47, 70, 129, 138. *See also* Commando Solo and aircraft
ECOMICI, 115–16, 119. *See also* ECOWAS Mission in Côte d'Ivoire, ECOWAS, and Economic Community of West African States
Economic Community of West African States, 46, 115, 125. *See also* ECOWAS, ECOWAS Mission in Côte d'Ivoire, and ECOMICI
ECOWAS, 46, 101, 106, 113, 115–16, 119–20, 122–23, 125, 131. *See also* Economic Community of West African States, ECOWAS Mission in Côte d'Ivoire, and ECOMICI
ECOWAS Mission in Côte d'Ivoire, 115. *See also* ECOMICI, ECOWAS, and Economic Community of West African States
Egal, Muhammad Ibrahim, 26
Entebbe, Uganda, 71
Escadrille de Transport 2.64, Armée l'Air, 134. *See also* French Air Force Transport Squadron 2.64 and ET 2.64
ET 2.64, 134. *See also Escadrille de Transport 2.64, Armée l'Air*, and French Air Force Transport Squadron 2.64
Ethiopia, 22–23, 28, 40
ethnic cleansing, 6, 15–16, 112, 125
EUCOM, 46. *See also* US European Command
European Union, 114
Eye of the People, 111. *See also L'Oeil du Peuple*

failed state, 21, 33, 39–41
Fédération Estudiantine et Scolaire de Côte d'Ivoire, 112. See also Côte d'Ivoire Student Federation and FESCI
Feil, Scott, 68
Fennec light helicopter, 134. See also aircraft and helicopters
FESCI, 112. See also *Fédération Estudiantine et Scolaire de Côte d'Ivoire* and Côte d'Ivoire Student Federation
5th French Army Aviation Combat Helicopter Regiment, 134. See also *5me Régiment d'Hélicoptères de Combat, Aviation Légère de L'Armée de Terre* and 5 RHC
Final Solution, 10–11, 53, 78
5 RHC, 134. See also *5me Régiment d'Hélicoptères de Combat, Aviation Légère de L'Armée de Terre* and 5th French Army Aviation Combat Helicopter Regiment
FPI, 105, 111–12. See also *Front Populaire Ivoirien* and Ivorian Popular Front
France, 34, 60–61, 68–70, 101, 103, 105–7, 112–17, 119–20, 123–24, 129, 131, 134
French Air Force Transport Squadron 2.64, 134. See also *Escadrille de Transport 2.64, Armée l'Air* and ET 2.64
French Special Operations Command, 134. See also *Commandement des Opérations Spéciales* and COS
Front Populaire Ivoirien, 105. See also Ivorian Popular Front and FPI

Gbagbo, Laurent, 105, 107, 111–12
gendarmerie, 105, 110
gendarmes, 111
General Accounting Office, 25
Genghis Khan, 9
genocidaires, 129
genocide, 1–19, 21–22, 27, 36, 45, 47, 53–54, 59, 61–69, 71–72, 75, 77–101, 108–10, 113, 117–25, 127–33, 136, 138, 140–41
Genocide Convention Implementation Act, 5
Genocide Intervention Network, 10, 18
Genocide Prevention Task Force, 3, 16, 18
Genocide Watch, 1–2, 10, 14, 17, 19, 99, 108, 125, 130

Georgetown University, 2
German, 4, 9–10, 29, 55, 77
Germany, 4, 46, 55, 72, 133, 137
Global Hawk RQ-4 UAV, 136. See also aircraft and UAV
Global Peace Operations Initiative, 46
global war on terror, 21, 36
Goude, Blé 117
Great Britain, 21
Great Leap Forward, 6
Guéï, Robert, 105–6, 114
Guinea, 102
Gulu, Uganda, 71

Habr Gedir subclan, 23
Habyarimana, Agathe, 86
Habyarimana, Juvenal, 78, 86
Harff, Barbara, 14
Hargeysa, Somalia, 23
Harrier AV-8, 140. See also aircraft
Harvard University, 16, 81
Harvard University, Carr Center for Human Rights Policy, 16. See also Carr Center for Human Rights Policy, Harvard University
helicopters, 7, 33–34, 43, 45, 66, 69, 97, 114, 131, 133–34, 136, 140–41
  AH-1, 34, 43
  AH-6, 43
  CH-47, 134
  Fennec (Puma) light helicopter, 134
  MH-60, 43
  SA.330 Cougar helicopters, 134
Helland, Sam, 35
Henry L. Stimson Center, 16, 19
Herbst, Jeffrey, 82
Hezbollah, 82
Hilberg, Raul, 1, 10–14
Hoar, Joseph P., 31
Holocaust, 1, 4, 10–11, 16, 84, 140
Horn-of-Africa, 28
Houphouët-Boigny, Felix, 103–4
Howe, Jonathan, 33–34
Human Rights Watch, 10, 80, 93, 111, 124–25, 130
Hutu, 6, 13, 54–65, 67, 72, 74, 77–78, 80–82, 86–89, 91–92, 94, 97–98, 136, 139
Hutu Social Movement, 58. See also *Mouvement Social Muhutu* and MSM
Hyde, Henry, 3

ibyitso, 62
ICRC, 29. *See also* International Committee of the Red Cross
igitero, 86–87, 99
Impuzamugambi, 88, 130
Indonesia, 6
Indonesian, 8
intelligence, surveillance, and reconnaissance, 47, 122. *See also* ISR
Intelligent Young African, 112. *See also Jeune Afrique L'Intelligent*
Interahamwe, 64–65, 68, 88, 130
International Commission on Intervention and State Sovereignty, 15
International Committee of the Red Cross, 29. *See also* ICRC
International Criminal Tribunal for Rwanda, 6
International Criminal Tribunal for the Former Yugoslavia, 5
international law, 4, 7, 80
intervention, 2, 7, 10, 15–17, 21–22, 25, 27–31, 33–39, 41, 43–45, 53, 66–67, 69–70, 72, 75, 79–83, 91, 93–95, 97–98, 101, 113, 118–23, 127–41
inyenzi, 60
Iraq, 4, 21, 39, 44, 67, 71, 132–33, 136–37, 139, 142
Iraqi, 46, 51, 71, 133
Isaaq clan, 23
ISR, 122, 132, 135–36. *See also* intelligence, surveillance, and reconnaissance
Italy, 21, 34
"Ivorian miracle," 102
Ivoirité, 103–5, 113, 118
Ivorian-born, 105
Ivorians, 103–4, 112
Ivorian Popular Front, 105. *See also Front Populaire Ivoirien* and FPI
Ivorian Popular Movement for the Great West, 106. *See also Mouvement Populaire Ivoirien du Grand Ouest* and MPIGO
Ivorian Television Broadcasting, 110. *See also Radiodiffusion Télévision Ivoirienne* and RTI
Ivory Coast, 101, 103

J-3/Operations, 30. *See also* Joint Staff and JS
J-5/Plans, 30. *See also* Joint Staff and JS

JCS, 30, 41. *See also* Joint Chiefs of Staff
Jean-Pierre, 68
Jeune Afrique L'Intelligent, 112. *See also Intelligent Young African*
Jews, 1, 4, 8, 10–13, 17, 19, 85
Johnston, Robert B., 32–33
Joint Chiefs of Staff, 30. *See also* JCS
Joint Staff, 28, 30. *See also* JS
Joint Task Force-Operation Provide Relief, 29. *See also* JTF-OPR
JS, 28, 30. *See also* Joint Staff
JTF-OPR, 29. *See also* Joint Task Force-Operation Provide Relief

Kangura, 63. *See also Wake Them Up*
Kavaruganda, Joseph, 65
Kennedy, Kevin, 42
Kenya, 1, 29
Khmer Rouge, 6, 8
Kibuye Province, Rwanda, 65
Kigali, Rwanda, 60–61, 63, 65, 68, 70–71, 84, 137
Kigali International Airport, 70
Kosovo, 1, 6, 15, 97, 123, 133
Kulaks, 8
Kuperman, Alan J., 69, 129
Kurdish, 132, 139

Landstuhl Regional Medical Center, Germany, 137
Lantos, Tom, 3
Lawrence College, 82
League of Nations, 4
Lemkin, Raphael, 3–4, 6, 10–11, 78
Liddell Hart, B. H., 82
Lieberman, Joseph, 3
Linas-Marcoussis Accord, 106. *See also* LMA
LMA, 106–7, 116. *See also* Linas-Marcoussis Accord
L'Oeil du Peuple, 111. *See also Eye of the People*
Lvov, Ukraine, 3

Mali, 102
man-portable air defense system, 136. *See also* MANPADS
MANPADS, 136. *See also* man-portable air defense system
Mao Tse-tung, 6

INDEX

mass killing, 2–4, 9–10, 14–15, 22, 24, 32, 37, 39, 68, 108, 118, 120–21, 127, 140
mass murder, 7, 9, 18, 83, 93, 98–99
MDR-PARMEHUTU, 58–59. *See also Mouvement Démocratique Républicain-Parti du Mouvement de l'Emancipation du Peuple Hutu* and Democratic Republican Movement-Party of the Movement for Emancipation of the Hutu People
MEDEVAC, 132, 136. *See also* medical evacuation
medical evacuation, 70, 132, 136–37. *See also* MEDEVAC
Mendez, Juan E., 110, 121
MH-60, 43
Mills, Nicholas, 82
Minority Rights Group International, 108
MINUCI, 106–7, 116–17, 120. *See also Mission des Nations Unies en Côte d'Ivoire* and UN Mission in Côte d'Ivoire
Mission des Nations Unies en Côte d'Ivoire, 106. *See also* UN Mission in Côte d'Ivoire and MINUCI
mistake of 1960, 60
MJP, 106. *See also Mouvement pour la Justice et la Paix* and Movement for Justice and Peace
Mogadishu, Somalia, 21, 23, 26–28, 34–35, 37–38, 43–44, 80
Mohamed, Ali Mahdi, 23, 26
Mombasa, Kenya, 29
Monoko-Zohi, Côte d'Ivoire, 111
Montreal Institute for Genocide and Human Rights Studies, 2, 17
Mouvement Démocratique Républicain-Parti du Mouvement de l'Emancipation du Peuple Hutu, 58. *See also* Democratic Republican Movement-Party of the Movement for Emancipation of the Hutu People and MDR-PARMEHUTU
Mouvement Patriotique de Côte d'Ivoire, 106. *See also* Patriotic Movement of Côte d'Ivoire and MPCI
Mouvement Populaire Ivoirien du Grand Ouest, 106. *See also* Ivorian Popular Movement for the Great West and MPIGO

Mouvement pour la Justice et la Paix, 106. *See also* Movement for Justice and Peace and MJP
Mouvement Révolutionaire Nationale pour le Développement, 88. *See also* National Revolutionary Movement for Development and MRND
Mouvement Social Muhutu, 58. *See also* Hutu Social Movement and MSM
Movement for Justice and Peace, 106. *See also Mouvement pour la Justice et la Paix* and MJP
MPCI, 106. *See also Mouvement Patriotique de Côte d'Ivoire* and Patriotic Movement of Côte d'Ivoire
MPIGO, 106. *See also Mouvement Populaire Ivoirien du Grand Ouest* and Ivorian Popular Movement for the Great West
MRND, 88. *See also Mouvement Révolutionaire Nationale pour le Développement* and National Revolutionary Movement for Development
MSM, 58. *See also* Hutu Social Movement and MSM
Museveni, Yoweri, 60
Muslim, 1, 101–6, 110–11, 124
MV-22 Osprey, 134. *See also* aircraft

National Resistance Army, 60
National Revolutionary Movement for Development, 88. *See also Mouvement Révolutionaire Nationale pour le Développement* and MRND
National Security Council, 6, 28. *See also* NSC
National Security Strategy, 2, 17, 21, 47, 121, 125, 141
nation-building, 21, 34
Native Americans, 1
NATO, 6, 80, 120, 123, 131–32
Natsios, Andrew, 3, 18
Nazi, 3–4, 10–11
Ndadaye, Melchior, 62, 64, 71
neoconservative, 9
New Forces, 106–7, 116
NSC, 28, 30, 34. *See also* National Security Council
NSC Deputies Committee, 30, 34. *See also* National Security Council and NSC
Nuremberg Trials, 4
nyumbakumi, 87–88

166

Oakley, Robert, 32, 66
OAU, 25. *See also* Organization of African Unity
Office of Cambodian Genocide Investigations, 2
Office of the Secretary of Defense, 28. *See also* OSD
Ogaden Region of Ethiopia, 22
193d Special Operations Wing, 138
ONUCI FM, 117, 138. *See also* Opération des Nations Unies en Côte d'Ivoire frequency modulated radio, UN Operation in Côte d'Ivoire, and UNOCI
Operation Allied Force, 71–72, 80, 83
Opération des Nations Unies en Côte d'Ivoire frequency modulated radio, 117. *See also* ONUCI FM, UN Operation in Côte d'Ivoire, and UNOCI
Operation Licorne, 114–16, 131, 134
Operation Provide Relief, 29, 37, 49
Operation Restore Hope, 30–32, 36, 41, 45, 50, 66, 82
Operation Turquoise, 69, 129
Organization of African Unity, 25. *See also* OAU
OSD, 28, 39. *See also* Office of the Secretary of Defense
Ouattara, Alassane, 104–6

Pakistan, 6
Pancrace, 65
Parti Democratique de la Côte d'Ivoire, 103. *See also* Democratic Party of Côte d'Ivoire and PDCI
Patriotic Movement of Côte d'Ivoire, 106. *See also Mouvement Patriotique de Côte d'Ivoire* and MPCI
PDCI, 103–5. *See also Parti Democratique de la Côte d'Ivoire* and Democratic Party of Côte d'Ivoire
peace-enforcement, 31, 33, 39, 127, 132, 136–38
Peacekeeping and Stability Operations Institute, 16. *See also* US Army Peacekeeping and Stability Operations Institute
Poland, 4
politicide, 8–10, 15
Polish, 3
Powell, Colin, 7, 30–31, 34

power, 2, 17–18, 21–25, 27–28, 30, 32–33, 37, 40–41, 44, 55–57, 62, 65, 78, 81, 86, 94, 96, 98–99, 102–4, 109–11, 114, 118, 121, 142
pregenocide, 77, 91
Presidential Decision Directive 25, 36
Prevent Genocide International, 10, 19, 101, 108
Princeton University, 82
Proxmire, William, 5–6
Puma helicopter, 134. *See also* aircraft and helicopters

R2P, 14–16, 19. *See also* responsibility to protect
Radio Télévision Libre Mille Collines, 63. *See also* Thousand Hills Independent Radio and Television and RTLMC
Radiodiffusion Télévision Ivoirienne, 110. *See also* Ivorian Television Broadcasting and RTI
Ramstein AB, Germany, 133
RANU, 60. *See also* Rwandese Alliance for National Unity
rapid genocide intervention, 79, 83, 130. *See also* RGI
Rassemblement des Républicains, 104. *See also* Republican Rally and RDR
RDR, 104–5, 110–11. *See also Rassemblement des Républicains* and Republican Rally
Reagan, Ronald, 5
realism, 79–80
Red Berets, 22–23
Red Cross, 10, 29, 137
Refugees International, 2, 63, 137
Reporters Without Borders, 110
republican, 2–3, 58, 104, 141
Republican Rally, 104. *See also Rassemblement des Républicains* and RDR
responsibility to protect, 14–16, 19. *See also* R2P
RGI, 79, 83–86, 90, 93–98, 130–31. *See also* rapid genocide intervention
Roman Catholic, 57
Roosevelt, 140
RPF, 60–65, 69–71, 78, 81, 87–88, 92, 95, 135. *See also* Rwandan Patriotic Front
RQ-1 Predator UAV, 47. *See also* aircraft, unmanned aerial vehicles, and UAV

INDEX

RTI, 110. *See also Radiodiffusion Télévision Ivoirienne* and Ivorian Television Broadcasting
RTLMC, 63–65, 70. *See also Radio Télévision Libre Mille Collines* and Thousand Hills Independent Radio and Television
Rummel, R. J., 8–9
Russian Empire, 3
Rwanda, 1, 6, 15, 36, 53–65, 67–75, 77, 80–82, 84, 86–87, 89, 92–93, 95–100, 108, 118–20, 123–25, 128–29, 132, 136, 138, 141
Rwandan Killing Machine, 78, 86–87, 89–90, 93, 97
Rwandan Patriotic Front, 60. *See also* RPF
Rwandese, 58, 60, 63
Rwandese Alliance for National Unity, 60. *See also* RANU
Rwandese National Union, 58. *See also Union Nationale Rwandaise* and UNAR
Rwandese Refugee Welfare Foundation, 60

SA.330 Cougar helicopters, 134. *See also* aircraft and helicopters
Sahnoun, Mohamed, 25–28, 48
Semitic, 55
Senate, 3, 5, 17
Serbia, 71
Serbian, 133
786th Expeditionary Squadron, 133
Shia, 139
Shoah, 1
SNA, 33–34, 43. *See also* Somali National Alliance
SNF, 24. *See also* Somali National Front
SNM, 23. *See also* Somali National Movement
Somali, 22–30, 33–36, 39–42, 48, 128, 139
Somali Air Force, 23
Somali National Alliance, 33, 139. *See also* SNA
Somali National Front, 24. *See also* SNF
Somali National Movement, 23. *See also* SNM
Somalia, 3, 15, 21–32, 35–44, 47–50, 66–67, 72, 75, 80, 82, 128, 136, 139
Somaliland, 26
Sosa, Juan Saúl, 70
Soviets, 4, 8
Special Envoy to Sudan, 3
Srebrenica, Bosnia, 1, 6, 15, 135
Stalinist, 8
STAND, 2, 64, 88, 94, 96–97, 105. *See also* Student Anti-Genocide Coalition and Students Taking Action Now: Darfur
Stanton, Gregory, 2, 12–14, 19, 98, 131
Student Anti-Genocide Coalition, 17. *See also* Students Taking Action Now: Darfur and STAND
sub-Saharan, 44
Sudan, 3, 6, 77, 123, 141
Suharto, 6
Sûreté Nationale, 110
Sweden, 4

Tanzania, 59–60
Task Force Ranger, 34–35
The Hague, 80
Thousand Hills Independent Radio and Television, 63. *See also Radio Télévision Libre Mille Collines* and RTLMC
Times (London), 112
TRAFIPRO, 58. *See also Travail, Fidélité, Progrès*
Travail, Fidélité, Progrès, 58. *See also* TRAFIPRO
Tutsi, 8, 54–65, 67–69, 72, 77–78, 81–82, 84, 86, 88–89, 91–92, 94, 98–99, 129, 139, 141
Twa, 54, 56, 58

UAV, 136. *See also* aircraft and unmanned aerial vehicles
Uganda, 59–61, 71, 96, 137
UN, 6–7, 15, 18, 26–36, 38–40, 43, 47–50, 53, 56–59, 65–66, 80, 103, 106–10, 116–18, 120–21, 124–25, 127–28, 132–35
UN African Union Mission in Darfur, 133. *See also* UNAMID
UN Assistance Mission in Rwanda, 53, 65. *See also* UNAMIR
UN Charter Chapter VI, 15, 28, 45. *See also* chapter VI, Charter of the United Nations
UN Charter Chapter VII, 15, 31, 33, 39, 68, 116. *See also* chapter VII, Charter of the United Nations
UN Committee on the Elimination of Racial Discrimination, 109. *See also* Committee on the Elimination of Racial Discrimination and CERD
UN expert on Genocide, 108

INDEX

UN General Assembly, 4–5, 67
UN High Commission on Refugees, 27. *See also* UNHCR
UN Mission in Côte d'Ivoire, 106. *See also Mission des Nations Unies en Côte d'Ivoire* and MINUCI
UN Observer Mission Uganda-Rwanda, 65. *See also* UNAMUR
UN Operation in Côte d'Ivoire, 107. *See also* UNOCI, *Opération des Nations Unies en Côte d'Ivoire* frequency modulated radio, and ONUCI FM
UN Operation in Somalia 27. *See also* UNOSOM
UN Operation in Somalia II, 31. *See also* UNOSOM II
UN Security Council Resolution 751, 27. *See also* UNSCR 751
UN Security Council Resolution 794. 31. *See also* UNSCR 794
UN Security Council Resolution 814, 33. *See also* UNSCR 814
UN Security Council Resolution 837, 33. *See also* UNSCR 837
UN Security Council Resolution 1769, 7. *See also* UNSCR 1769
UN Special Advisor on the Prevention of Genocide, 110
UN World Food Program, 27. *See also* UNWFP
UNAMID, 7, 133–34. *See also* UN African Union Mission in Darfur
UNAMIR, 53, 66–68, 135. *See also* UN Assistance Mission in Rwanda
UNAMUR, 65. *See also* UN Observer Mission Uganda-Rwanda
UNAR, 58–59. *See also Union Nationale Rwandaise* and Rwandese National Union
UNHCR, 27. *See also* UN High Commission on Refugees
Unified Task Force, 31. *See also* UNITAF
Union Nationale Rwandaise, 58. *See also* Rwandese National Union and UNAR
UNITAF, 31–33, 37–42, 66, 128. *See also* Unified Task Force
United Nations, 2, 4–7, 15, 18–19, 21–22, 25–28, 31–35, 37–39, 43–45, 53, 59, 63, 65–66, 68, 72, 81–83, 94–95, 101, 106–8, 113, 116–21, 123–25, 133–34, 136, 141
United Nations Genocide Convention, 22
United Somali Congress, 23. *See also* USC
United States, 1–2, 4–6, 10, 16–17, 19, 25–26, 34, 38–40, 44, 46–50, 53, 67–68, 72, 81–82, 101, 115, 121–23, 125, 131–33, 137–39, 141
United States Holocaust Memorial Museum, 1, 16–17, 19. *See also* USHMM
University of Wisconsin, 77
unmanned aerial vehicles, 136. *See also* aircraft and UAV
UNOCI, 107, 116–17, 119–20, 125, 131. *See also* UN Operation in Côte d'Ivoire, *Opération des Nations Unies en Côte d'Ivoire* frequency modulated radio, and ONUCI FM
UNOSOM, 27–28, 30–38, 40, 43, 66, 128. *See also* UN Operation in Somali
UNOSOM II, 31–35, 37–38, 40, 43, 66, 128. *See also* UN Operation in Somalia II
UNSCR 751, 27. *See also* UN Security Council Resolution 751
UNSCR 794, 31. *See also* UN Security Council Resolution 794
UNSCR 814, 33. *See also* UN Security Council Resolution 814
UNSCR 837, 33. *See also* UN Security Council Resolution 837
UNSCR 1769, 7. *See also* UN Security Council Resolution 1769
UNWFP, 27. *See also* UN World food Program
US, 2–7, 10, 12, 14, 16, 18, 21–22, 25, 28–37, 39, 41–44, 46–47, 49, 51, 53, 65–66, 69, 79–82, 96, 121–23, 127–28, 131–39, 141
US Africa Command, 46. *See also* US AFRICOM
US AFRICOM, 46–47. *See also* US Africa Command
US Air Force, 29, 131–35, 138
US Army Peacekeeping and Stability Operations Institute, 16
US Army Special Forces, 34
US Central Command, 29
US European Command, 46, 51. *See also* EUCOM
US National Command Authority, 35
US National Defense Strategy, 36

INDEX

USAF, 21, 29, 53, 77. *See also* US Air Force
USC, 23–24, 34. *See also* United Somali Congress
USHMM, 1, 10, 17–18. *See also* United States Holocaust Memorial Museum
USNS *Comfort*, 137
USNS *Mercy*, 137
Uwilingiyimana, 65–66
Uzbekistan, 1

Valentino, Benjamin, 18, 47–48, 78, 98

Wake Them Up, 63. *See also Kangura*
Wehrmacht, 4
Weinberger (Caspar) doctrine, 79
Work, Fidelity, Progress, 58. *See also Travail, Fidélité, Progrès* and TRAFIPRO

Yale University's Genocide Studies Program, 2, 17
Young Patriots, 113, 117

Zaire, 60, 69–70, 96
Zimbabwe, 1, 99

Stopping Mass Killings in Africa
Genocide, Airpower, and Intervention

Air University Press Team

Chief Editor
Jim Howard

Copy Editor
Darlene H. Barnes

Cover Art and Book Design
Steven C. Garst

Illustrations
L. Susan Fair

*Composition and
Prepress Production*
Ann Bailey

Quality Review
Mary J. Moore

Print Preparation
Joan Hickey

Distribution
Diane Clark

This page is intentionally left blank.

www.ingramcontent.com/pod-product-compliance
Lightning Source LLC
Chambersburg PA
CBHW080505110426
42742CB00017B/3005